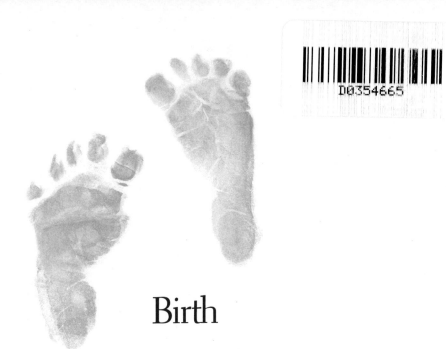

Birth

Birth

A Literary Companion

EDITED BY KRISTIN KOVACIC
AND LYNNE BARRETT

University of Iowa Press Ψ Iowa City

University of Iowa Press, Iowa City 52242
Printed in the United States of America

Design by Erin Kirk New

http://www.uiowa.edu/uiowapress

The publication of this book was generously supported by the University
of Iowa Foundation.

Printed on acid-free paper

Library of Congress Cataloging-in-Publication Data
Birth: a literary companion / edited by Kristin Kovacic and Lynne Barrett.
     p.   cm.
   Includes index.
   ISBN 0-87745-831-6 (pbk.)
     1. Childbirth—Literary collections.   2. Parent and child—Literary
collections.   3. American literature—20th century.   4. Parenting—
Literary collections.   I. Kovacic, Kristin, 1963–.   II. Barrett, Lynne,
1950–.

PS509.C5154 B47   2002
810.8'0354—dc21   2002021136

02   03   04   05   06   P   5   4   3   2   1

For James, Ramsey, and Rosalie

Contents

Introduction   xi

First Stirrings

Genesis 1:28   *Kate Daniels*   3

First Pregnancy   *Gary Metras*   5

Letter in July   *Elizabeth Spires*   6

Heartbeat   *Laurie Kutchins*   8

Upon Seeing an Ultrasound Photo of an Unborn Child   *Thomas Lux*   9

First Stirrings   *Rosemary Bray*   10

Cleaning the Pheasant in the Fifth Month of My Wife's Pregnancy
Harry Humes   14

You're   *Sylvia Plath*   15

Reading the *New York Times*   *Jeanne Murray Walker*   16

Before   *Mary Grimm*   17

Delphos, Ohio   *Campbell McGrath*   28

Eighteenth-Century Medical Illustration: The Infant in Its Little
Room   *Ann Townsend*   31

Listening   *David Mura*   33

This Night   *Cathy Song*   35

Requiem   *Lia Purpura*   36

You Have the Body   *Elyse Gasco*   38

Notes from the Delivery Room

My Mother Gives Birth   *Julianna Baggott*   55

Transition   *Toi Derricotte*   56

from *Still Life*   A. S. Byatt   61

Women's Labors   *Lee Upton*   67

Notes from the Delivery Room   *Linda Pastan*   69

Giving Birth   *Margaret Atwood*   70

After Giving Birth, I Recall the Madonna and Child   *Julianna Baggott*   84

Delivering Lily   *Phillip Lopate*   85

Child of the Sun—Gabriel's Birth (Sun Prayer)   *Jimmy Santiago Baca*   101

Birth Report   *Stephen Dobyns*   104

Waiting   *Lisa Lenzo*   106

Ancestral Lights   *Deborah Digges*   113

The First Day   *Elizabeth Spires*   115

How It Begins   *David Mura*   117

Holding Bernadette   *Hunt Hawkins*   118

Milk   *Eileen Pollack*   120

For Fathers of Girls   *Stephen Dunn*   138

The Welcoming

Coming Home from the Hospital after My Son's Birth   *Jim Daniels*   143

The Welcoming   *Edward Hirsch*   144

Shrinking the Uterus   *Cathy Song*   148

Her First Week   *Sharon Olds*   150

Babylove   *Corinne Demas*   151

The Man Who Would Be a Mother   *Herbert Scott*   155

from *The Velveteen Father*   *Jesse Green*   156

Apnea   *Hunt Hawkins*   163

Gas   *Belle Waring*   164

Changing Diapers   *Gary Snyder*   165

Babyshit Serenade   *Alicia Ostriker*   166

Sleep   *Gary Krist*   167

from *Domestic Interior*   *Eavan Boland*   179

Morning Song   *Sylvia Plath*   181

Sorrow   *Ann Townsend*   182

New Mother   *Sharon Olds*   183

The Waiting   *Li-Young Lee*   184

Ménage à trois   *Kate Daniels*   188

Breastfeeding in Indiana   *Jane McCafferty*   189

March   *Jim Daniels*   199

First Summer   *Laurie Kutchins*   201

Now That I Am Forever with Child

Little Sleep's-Head Sprouting Hair in the Moonlight   *Galway Kinnell*   207

Brown Circle   *Louise Glück*   213

Simple Joys   *Quincy Troupe*   215

Motherhood   *Rita Dove*   216

Propaganda Poem: Maybe for Some Young Mamas   *Alicia Ostriker*   217

Saul and Patsy Are in Labor   *Charles Baxter*   223

Gravity *Kim Addonizio* 239

Orangutan Means Orange Man *Deborah Digges* 240

Prayer for My Children *Kate Daniels* 242

Now That I Am Forever with Child *Audre Lorde* 243

Contributors 245

Permissions 251

Index 257

Introduction

Parenthood is full of secrets. The pregnant body, labor itself, the mysteries of the new child, the transformation in our relationships — men and women are themselves reborn as they go through the process of becoming parents. It's almost beyond language, this becoming. As we went through pregnancy and the births of our children, we sought the truth of what was happening to us and what was about to happen. We were *bombarded* by language: common wisdom from family, friends, and strangers; questions from colleagues suddenly empowered to discuss our breasts and cervixes; and the new gospels of medicine. We took it all in. We went to Lamaze. We committed *What to Expect When You're Expecting* to memory. But we felt, finally, as Margaret Atwood's laboring mother does in her short story, "Giving Birth," that we were not prepared: "She realizes she has practiced for the wrong thing. A. squeezing her knee was nothing, she should have practiced for this, whatever it is."

This, whatever it is. When Lynne was pregnant, she found that, though certainly some of what she learned was useful, it never seemed to be enough. The factual books offered a tour of all possible ills and errors, but somehow didn't convey the experience she was facing. And many friends seemed unable or unwilling to tell a detailed truth about it — or, chasing their own kids around, they hardly had time.

She remembered that Mary McCarthy's *The Group* had a chapter on breast-feeding and reread it, discovering that, though written in a different time, it showed the political battlefield the breast was to become. So she laughed (and worried) with McCarthy, and hugged it to her, as people around her extolled breastfeeding (Hey, guess what, at the start it really hurts! It doesn't just come naturally!). Reading A. S. Byatt's *Still Life*, too, she found a wonderful narrative of pregnancy and birth, of the life of the body and of the mind. But all she managed to locate was these two books, and they didn't fully satisfy her hunger for detailed description and the deep companionship reading affords. Perhaps, she thought, no one out there is telling the truth.

When Lynne's son was a year old, Kristin became pregnant, and Lynne re-solved to be as truthful as possible about childbirth, its terrors as well as its joys, and the two of us enjoyed sharing our stories. Kristin found herself scanning the biographical notes on book jackets for evidence of parenthood, searching for more allies in this new emotional terrain. In this way she found Lee Upton's "Women's Labors" and Edward Hirsch's "The Welcoming," poems she treas-ures more than the photos of her first newborn. (They're more accurate, recall-ing *her* emotions exactly.) Some time later, after Kristin had her second child, she suggested we work together to make the book we wished existed. And we discovered that there had been a flood of truth telling in the interim, as a gen-eration of writers broke the taboo on this experience, more secret than sex.

That's how this book was born. Like Stephanie in Byatt's *Still Life*, who asks only for her copy of Wordsworth in the labor room, we feel strongly that no one should go through birth without the company of literature. (If worse comes to worst, you can read the words aloud; it keeps you breathing!) Au-thentic, specific, and grounded in emotional truth, a well-crafted poem, story, or essay can unlock the secrets that science and society never reveal. "What pain?" Atwood's laboring mother, Jeannie, thinks: "When there is no pain she feels nothing, when there is pain, she feels nothing because there is no *she*. This, finally, is the disappearance of language. *You don't remember afterwards*, she has been told by almost everyone."

Our aim was to construct an imaginative guide, not to the biological drama of birth (although many of the writers we found make useful, exacting de-scriptions of this), but to the emotional and spiritual changes parenthood brings on. Our criteria for selecting work were simple. We asked, "What would we and our partners have liked to read as we went through the births of our children? What would have been comforting, illuminating, important to know?" We searched for work that covered the huge emotional spectrum we knew parenting to be, from fear and loathing to uncontainable joy. Above all, we looked for concrete expressions of the birth experience, clear and full of specific detail, to take the place of the abstract, often sentimental, popular rep-resentations of motherhood or fatherhood that make every parent feel like a "bad" one.

To our pleasure, we found there was real writing out there, work with the mix of terror, comedy, irritation, and lyricism we know to be the truth of becoming a parent. Much of this work came from writers we already admired, whom we would read on any subject. Several pieces, such as Galway Kinnell's "Little Sleep's-Head Sprouting Hair in the Moonlight," Audre Lorde's "Now That I Am Forever with Child," and Sylvia Plath's poems, are already quite well known, and we've included them here to be available to a reader at the moment they're most necessary. We of course turned to Sharon Olds and Alicia Ostriker, poets working in the tradition of Plath to articulate the female experience. Some writers, we discovered, had been mining the subject of birth over whole books of poems and stories: Julianna Baggott, Kate Daniels, Toi Derricotte, Elyse Gasco, Hunt Hawkins, Laurie Kutchins, Lia Purpura, Cathy Song, Elizabeth Spires, and Jeanne Murray Walker among them.

Perhaps we've begun to identify a new literary genre: birth literature. Like war for literary generations past, this genre has its conventions—the heroic labor room battle, the middle-of-the-night feeding—and its masters, among whom Plath and Olds and others among our contributors must be counted. Our search was not exhaustive, and there are doubtless many fine pieces we've overlooked. We hope this book inspires readers to seek out, and perhaps write themselves, work in this new tradition.

We combined poetry and prose, short and long pieces, with the idea that the book can be read solidly or dipped into in the middle of the night. We also liked the range of structure and tone that multiple genres provide. Poems offer images and meaningful moments; they shape and contain the ephemeral, as when Sylvia Plath describes the unborn child in "You're": "Vague as fog and looked for like mail." In tone, we found, particularly on this subject, poems tend toward wonder and reverence. Prose can create an experience in "real time," extremely useful, for example, for evoking labor or a newborn night (see "Delivering Lily" by Phillip Lopate and "Sleep" by Gary Krist), when time itself becomes transformed. We were happy to find prose, like Jane McCafferty's "Breastfeeding in Indiana" and Mary Grimm's "Before," that veers into irony, ambivalence, even skepticism.

Among the mysteries of childbirth, the secrets of the sexes must be counted. Most books, we've found, deal exclusively with motherhood or fatherhood. Even casual information is often segregated, the gossip chain of moms or dads.

(In the gay community, as Jesse Green points out in *The Velveteen Father*, such a chain has to be painstakingly created, link by link.) We decided early on to include work from all sides, unlocking the secrets we hold from one another.

> He has a secret he has not told Patsy, though she probably knows it: he does not have any clue to being a parent. He does not love being one, though he loves his daughter with a newfound intensity close to hysteria. To him, fatherhood is one long unrewritable bourgeois script. Love, rage, and tenderness disable him in the chairs in which he sits, miming calm, holding Mary Esther. At night, when Patsy is fast asleep, Saul kneels on the landing and beats his fists on the stairs.
>
> —"Saul and Patsy Are in Labor," Charles Baxter

It's interesting to trace the fathers' voices through this book, from Gary Metras's curious observer in "First Pregnancy" to Jimmy Santiago Baca's awed participant in "Child of the Sun" to Hunt Hawkins's desperate caregiver in "Apnea." Next to these we set women's experiences, including Rosemary Bray's pregnant uncertainty in "First Stirrings," Toi Derricotte's illuminating pain in "Transition," and Corinne Demas's character's overwhelming fullness in "Babylove."

Much work here deals with the transformation a child brings to a relationship. In pieces such as Li-Young Lee's "The Waiting," Elyse Gasco's "You Have the Body," and Kate Daniels's "Ménage à trois," you'll find mothers looking at fathers and fathers looking at mothers, as they ask, Who am I? Who are you? Who will we become?

Although there are many kinds of parents in this book—married, single, gay, straight—and many kinds of births—"natural," medically assisted, adoptive, and biological—our aim in selecting work has not been to cover every possible experience or to advocate a particular method. In fact, some of the pieces included here mention birth practices that are no longer common in America. What we have tried to locate, in a variety of voices, is the thread that is continuous in the birth process, the central questions and changes everyone faces. We believe there is a language all parents speak, mostly to themselves.

But we also aim for this book to be practical. Like a traditional guidebook, *Birth* is organized chronologically, from early pregnancy to late infancy. New

First Stirrings

parents are inside a very real experience, and we think it's one of the uses of literature to be a thoughtful companion to life's realities, one we wish we'd had when our children were born. The book's centerpiece is a collection of interpretations of labor: a window, through art, to what it's *really* like.

All the work collected here is marked by its generous intention, which we share — to capture, for the benefit of those who follow, our own births as parents. We feel, as we read, the thrill of a writer truly getting it, of finally pinning an elusive experience down. We're grateful to the writers featured in this book for their honesty, courage, and faith in language. We're grateful to the book's early readers and believers: Lara Kovacic Cosentino, Nancy Koerbel, Cynthia Miller, Richard McDonough, and, for emotional and technical support, to Robert Morison, Jim Daniels, Lissette Mendez, and George Tucker. And we're grateful to our children, to whom this book is dedicated, for delivering us into a whole new world.

Kristin Kovacic and Lynne Barrett

Genesis 1:28

KATE DANIELS

In the dank clarity of the Green Line tunnel,
we hatched our plan — to grow a creature
from those nights of love, those afternoons
of thick scents, those liquid mornings, odor
of coffee mingling with musk. Actually, he wanted
six, he said, standing there in the chill, a train
thundering up like an epiphany the two of us
verified together.

I knew then it was over, irrevocably
over, my previous life, alone and unloved, could see
how it would finally play itself out, starring him
and our creatures, the chaotic kitchen, the rumpled
beds, my wrinkled shirttails smeared with egg.
Helplessly, I tilted toward him and those sweet
images, to his mouth and his smell, toward my life
and my future, the nights we would recline, locked
and rocking in groaning love, the months my belly
would expand with our efforts, the bloody bringing forth
of two of him and one of me.

I stood for one last moment alone,
inside a cloud of grace, a pure and empty
gift of space where history released its grip.
Its bulging bag of bad memories burst open
in the doors of a train and was carried off
to a distant city I swore never to revisit.
And then I turned to his lips and his tongue,
to our hands in our gloves unbuckling each other,

calculating how quickly we could travel
back home. To anyone watching, it must have
looked like lust — two lovers emboldened
by the anonymity residing in a subway stop.
What kind of being could possibly see
a new world was being made, a universe
created? Who could have known how called
we were to what we were doing? How godlike
it was, how delicious, how holy?

First Pregnancy

GARY METRAS

It is early evening.
She naps on the couch.
I sit in a corner of the room
outside her smile, her dreams.

Does she dream of which way
life will swish tonight?
Of futures with vowels, like butterflies,
almost within her grasp? Her lips
flutter briefly.

And the child, of guessed-at
hair and eye color, this twitch
of life nearing wholeness,
about to blink in a dark sea,
can it feel the setting sunlight
whisper to the mother, or is she just
a humid cave growing tighter?

The sun is incidental now, like the past,
an unheeded breeze
sinking in the weight
of its own revelations
as the inches sprout from within.

The corner deepens with night.
She sleeps in a trough of life.
I, in a chair, rock and stare.

Letter in July

ELIZABETH SPIRES

My life slows and deepens.
I am thirty-eight, neither here nor there.
It is a morning in July, hot and clear.
Out in the field, a bird repeats its quaternary call,
four notes insisting, *I'm here, I'm here.*
The field is unmowed, summer's wreckage everywhere.
Even this early, all is expectancy.

It is as if I float on a still pond,
drowsing in the bottom of a rowboat,
curled like a leaf into myself.
The water laps at its old wooden sides
as the sun beats down on my body,
a wand, an enchantment, shaping it
into something languid and new.

A year ago, two, I dreamed I held
a mirror to your unborn face and saw you,
in that warped, watery glass, not as a child
but as you will be twenty years from now.
I woke, a light breeze lifting the curtain,
as if touched by a ghost's thin hand,
light filling the room, coming from nowhere.

I know the time, the place of our meeting.
It will be January, the coldest night
of the year. You will be carrying a lantern
as you enter the world crying,
and I cry to hear you cry.
A moment that, even now,
I carry in my body.

Heartbeat

LAURIE KUTCHINS

My pants pushed down around my knees
as the nurse instructed, I regress to schoolgirl twitches.
My still-slim ankles clank the base of the padded
examination table, my fingers twist an unconscious fringe
in the sanitary paper sheet until the doorknob rolls
and the no-eye-contact ob/gyn enters this pink room.
Like a fan across the whole span of my stomach, he opens
his cold manly hand that smells of antiseptic and metal.
Did the boy-skin of his hands understand they could grow
this gnarled and large, did they fathom they would be touching
the bodies of women all day in such sexless ways?
At this stage, my skin cannot fathom stretching past a holiday feast,
rounding to the jump-ball shapes of expectant girls
I saw leave the clinic with cigarettes already in hand.
Where he first spread his palm, the doctor places the ear
of a stethoscope attached to a transistor box. He turns the dial
until the sound of an ocean comes to me, the water of my breath.
And faintly — inside the inside — I have to stop breathing to hear it —
   tictictictictictictictictictictictictictictic . . .
It's the end of the eighth week, the indifferent period I've read about,
when the labiascrota splits into two words, two worlds,
and I hear it pushing time like a dark clock,
this speck of abstract sex in the fluids,
this sound with its own plan.

Upon Seeing an Ultrasound Photo of an Unborn Child

THOMAS LUX

Tadpole, it's not time yet to nag you
about college (though I have some thoughts
on that), baseball (ditto), or abstract
principles. Enjoy your delicious,
soupy womb-warmth, do some rolls and saults
(it'll be too crowded soon), delight in your early
dreams—which no one will attempt to analyze.
For now: may your toes blossom, your fingers
lengthen, your sexual organs grow (too soon
to tell which yet) sensitive, your teeth
form their buds in their forming jawbone, your already
booming heart expand (literally
now, metaphorically later); O your spine,
eyebrows, nape, knees, fibulae,
lungs, lips . . . But your soul,
dear child: I don't see it here, when
does that come in, whence? Perhaps God,
and your mother, and even I—we'll all contribute
and you'll learn yourself to coax it
from wherever: your soul, which holds your bones
together and lets you live
on earth.—Fingerling, sidecar, nubbin,
I'm waiting, it's me, Dad,
I'm out here. You already know
where Mom is. I'll see you more directly
upon arrival. You'll recognize
me—I'll be the tall-seeming, delighted
blond guy, and I'll have
your nose.

First Stirrings

ROSEMARY BRAY

It is five A.M.; it doesn't matter which morning. For the past several months, there have been dozens of mornings in which I watch the sun's ascent through slivers of the venetian blinds in my bedroom. My husband lies next to me, snoring gently; I nudge him into turning on his side to sleep in silence. City birds are singing in a monotone, and the newspaper delivery truck has already rumbled up the street and gone. I shift my unwieldy body from one part of the hot sheet to another, yawning but unable to sleep; this is the second night in three that I haven't closed my eyes. I have a meeting in less than four hours; I'll be there, bleary and resentful. I turn over again, or try to; this time, the baby kicks me squarely in the bladder. Time to get up, to release the ten drops of urine I was sure would be a flood. I keep telling myself that it won't be long now, that he'll release me soon, stop crawling around inside me and prodding me when I sit hunched over in chairs. He'll be in my life forever, but perhaps at a distance I can deal with. Mostly, though, I curse under my breath every woman who perpetuates the lie of blissful fecundity. It's clear to me through the haze of sleeplessness that wanting a baby is one thing; wanting to HAVE a baby is quite another.

A decade ago, when my husband and I decided to marry, I got a host of reactions from friends and acquaintances. To my surprise, many of them were negative. People warned me of the dangers of losing myself, being taken over by my husband, being trapped by the institution of marriage itself. Some of these doomsayers were themselves married women, issuing their dismaying reports from the front, as it were. I did speak to a few happy couples, but not many. I decided to ignore the grim folks, for the most part — it was not as though Bob and I were strangers to each other before our wedding day. We would be happy; I would not lose myself; marriage would be hard, but not impossible.

I was right. I did not lose myself, but found instead more in me than I knew was there. It was hard, but not impossible; we were happy. So happy, in fact, that having a baby seemed the logical next step. We were happy enough to want more of us around. It took time; for a period of months when I swore I was infertile, I wept at the sight of a child or the first trickle of blood, angry with myself for being so unoriginal. Then we decided on adoption and my pain eased. We prepared ourselves for the inevitable invasion of privacy that would allow the agency to check us out. We went to orientations and did our first interview, which lasted four hours. Exactly nine days later, I stood in our slightly seedy, white-tiled bathroom, watching a big, pink plus sign appear in the window of a home pregnancy test. Bob was in the living room, watching the climax of an obscure Gregory Peck movie; I called to him and showed him the test, watched his expression turn from vague frustration to a bewildered delight.

"Oh, my God," he said, and laughed. We stared at the test resting on the edge of the pedestal sink, then stared at each other. "So, Merry Christmas two days late," I said, and started to cry. It was my last truly happy day for months.

My body and I have never been friends. Plagued with a weight problem since adolescence, awkward enough to have flunked gym in kindergarten, I tend to think of my body primarily as something to anchor my head, the place where the really important stuff is going on. Over the years, I have learned to be more gentle with myself, declaring between us a kind of truce in which I agree not to subject us to further bizarre diets and Spartan programs of torture; my body, in turn, agreed to function without causing me severe limitations. To make this deal, I gave up the public approval that comes with thinness and some of the energy that weighing less can bring. I gained, however, possession of my sanity. It seemed like a fair trade to me.

But my pregnancy ended our cease-fire; hormone after hormone stepped into the breach. Fewer than twenty-four hours after I learned the good news, my stomach responded with a dreaded nausea that abated only if I ate or slept. Bland food, the advertised salvation of pregnant women everywhere, made me even queasier. Only Szechuan food and ginger saved me. Even so, the relative license to eat that pregnant women take for granted did me little good. At a time when my doctor expected me to gain weight, I actually lost two pounds one month, as I discovered at a prenatal checkup. For nearly thirty-eight years I had waited not to be hungry. Now the moment was here — and it was the wrong moment.

Yet tests revealed that the baby and I were growing well and doing fine. But my body held even more surprises. One night, after showering, I was idly examining my breasts. Brushing against one nipple with a bare hand, I wondered why I felt damp when I had just finished drying off. I looked down to find small beads of clear fluid at a nipple's edge — my breasts were simply warming up for the work ahead, and I was secreting on schedule. The fear washing over me was startling. It was the fear of the inevitable, the steady progression of events that would lead me to the birth of another human being. That night in my bathroom, I wanted no part of it.

A few weeks later, I sat at my computer working. I felt a flutter, almost a tickle, low in my abdomen. Still concentrating on my task, I vaguely noted to myself that whatever I'd eaten was starting to talk back to me. But when it happened again, I realized it was not food sending me a message, but my son-in-progress. I had always heard that this was a magical moment for pregnant women: the first stirrings of new life, the "quickening" that made an amorphous blob of cells into YOUR son, YOUR daughter. But I didn't feel magical. I felt invaded, occupied by hostile forces. The very first picture I visualized was a scene from *Alien*, in which John Hurt is trying to eat his dinner with the rest of the crew, until he is gnawed to death from within by the hideous monster that exits from his stomach with a bloody snarl.

That flutter was good for an hour of miserable tears, with Bob doing his best to console me. But for days I was beyond consolation. I felt betrayed into nonexistence; this baby I had prayed for and longed for would not be joining my life, it seemed, but overtaking it all together. It was all I thought about, all anyone else thought about who knew me. I was in the grip of primordial fears. I had already begun to disappear. My slide into panic was not aided by many of those who had preceded me into parenthood; their idea of congratulating me consisted primarily of rueful laughter, followed by the knowing comments: "If there's something you really want to do, or somewhere you want to go, you'd better do it now!" or "Just wait! Your life will never be the same." The specter of impending motherhood had done what nearly ten years of marriage had never achieved: brought on a sense of being trapped. Had I discovered too late that this life of mine, which would never be the same, was a life that had made me happier than I thought?

Every twinge, every tickle, every new symptom my body created did nothing for a time except to remind me of my bondage. Even my mind began to fail me; a head that once was filled with opinions and ideas became instead a repository for dreamy scenes of me and the baby in the park, in his room, on the bus, or in the playground, surrounded by admirers of my perfect child, my awareness of the outside world gone forever. And when I was not mourning the imminent death of myself, or my marriage, I focused on the baby's safety, as though my traitorous thoughts might jeopardize his very life. Annoyed as I had been at his first stirrings inside me, I grew anxious every few hours that I could not feel him squirming.

Only the counsel of a few close friends saved me from a complete slide into hysteria. I relied on them, on their contrarious stories of how much they hated every waking moment of their pregnancies, that only the results — their own sweet-faced and self-possessed infants — justified the months of what they agreed was some version of hell. These women rescued me from my early terror of being an unnatural mother already plotting her escape from parenting, lost in the nightmare that I'd never write another word. The comment I cherished most came from my dear friend Renita, a professor and Old Testament scholar whose exquisite daughter, Savannah, was born nine months before my son. She made it her business to tell me to ignore everyone who talked about the end of my life. "Girl, pay these women no mind," she told me. "All these people who tell you what they can't do now that they have children — they weren't doing anything *before* they had kids."

Ultimately, though, it is harder to ignore my changing physical self. In these last days before my child's birth, muscles hurt that I didn't even know I possessed; all the old positions that once lulled me to sleep are useless. Sleep itself, something I could always count on, eludes me frequently. And the pleasures of sleeping next to someone warm have given way to the feeling that there are too many people in bed with me right now, a feeling I've refused to act upon on principle. For now, I am making Bob roll over more, while I try to find just one comfortable spot for a few hours of peace. It's plain that my son and I are already trying to find our way together. The mother-to-be in me imagines that love will cure the largest part of my dilemma. The writer in me considers it all one enormous metaphor. We will see.

Cleaning the Pheasant in the Fifth Month of My Wife's Pregnancy

HARRY HUMES

I cut through red and brown feathers,
down to the skin and layers of fat,
the crop full of corn.
Last night a neighbor said his grandfather
listens each evening to the radio
for the voice of his dead wife.
All around me a serious white weather
settles on bittersweet and corn stalk,
over the cardinal low in the holly.
I hang the pheasant in the shed,
then walk to the kitchen
with its smells of basil and sage,
and run water over my stained hands.
My wife's fingers touch the place
below her breasts where a small dance happens.
I go to the freezer and take out
the block of ice with the trout inside,
orange side spots and deep eyes,
back curved as though about to rise
for something we could not see.
Small pools of water form on the table.
Our fingers go numb tracing its shape.
Later we will watch the opossum
come out of the shadows to our porch.
We know the way it plays dead
when threatened, and how many
of its comma-shaped young fit into a teaspoon.
It comes to eat the cat's food.
It is the other mystery in the night.

You're

SYLVIA PLATH

Clownlike, happiest on your hands,
Feet to the stars, and moon-skulled,
Gilled like a fish. A common-sense
Thumbs-down on the dodo's mode.
Wrapped up in yourself like a spool,
Trawling your dark as owls do.
Mute as a turnip from the Fourth
Of July to All Fools' Day,
O high-riser, my little loaf.

Vague as fog and looked for like mail.
Farther off than Australia.
Bent-backed Atlas, our traveled prawn.
Snug as a bud and at home
Like a sprat in a pickle jug.
A creel of eels, all ripples.
Jumpy as a Mexican bean.
Right, like a well-done sum.
A clean slate, with your own face on.

Reading the *New York Times*

JEANNE MURRAY WALKER

You flutter for your life inside my belly,
swimming the quick stroke of the unborn
and I look up from making the morning toast,
reading the *New York Times*. I feel your splash
like the shiver of a tambourine
above the paper's cool, factual voice.
It numbers buried silos in North Dakota.
And today I can imagine them being fired.
First strike capability.
Equal to so many tons of TNT.
You flutter. The paper calculates how many
times each human being could die and this time
you must be counted. Our skin would sag like rotting
cloth, our eyebrows singe and crumble,
our faces be undressed to skulls together.
Above this voice reciting death
you bang your tambourine to tell me you are
growing eyes and toes. You're a parade.
You strike up the band and kick high for dear life.

Before

MARY GRIMM

I got pregnant on my honeymoon. We'd screwed everywhere we could for a year and three months, not using a blessed thing, so I had had this feeling that it was a matter of willpower — or not even willpower but just your body knowing that you were ready to settle into life. "Okay," the message would go from your brain down your backbone — *pow blip kazaam* — right to the ovaries: "It's time, *right now*," and things would release, open up. Your hands would fit themselves to — I don't know, knitting needles, diaper pins — your hair would start to grow itself into your mother's hairstyle, and you'd automatically stop wanting to go out and drink like a fool and dance all night. I figured this was going to happen when I was around twenty-six; I ought to have had nearly another six years. Oh, I planned to use birth control, I wasn't a total crazy. Just that once, though, just for that couple of days, we didn't want to waste time hanging out in a drugstore.

And, honestly, we were both embarrassed to go in and buy stuff. Now I slap those tubes of jelly on the counter along with the Hershey bars and ten-inch-fashion-doll clothes and corn plasters, and I don't give a damn. But then I didn't even like to see the little sign where the contraceptive stuff was kept that read FEMININE HYGIENE, as if potential babies were something to be scrubbed away. Some of the stuff said "Spermicide," too — something like an insect spray.

"You go," I'd say.

"No, you," Allen would say.

"I won't."

"You have to go," he'd say. "You promised, Bonnie."

"I did not."

And so on.

The upshot of this ignorance, this bashfulness, was a baby — or at first not the baby itself but its symptoms: a heavy burning ache behind my breastbone, an inability to stand toothpaste, the gradual swelling of my familiar body into a strange fruit — a gourd or a melon — from which my thin arms and legs stuck out like twigs.

This brought the relatives around to count backward from the due date and offer advice. Most Sundays Allen drove me to one house or another full of aunts, uncles, in-laws, cousins, family friends. I'd sit in big, soft chairs surrounded by people looking at my stomach, and I'd answer questions: "It's due in April" . . . "I'm going to work until the last month" . . . "As long as it's healthy."

Secretly, I wanted to have a girl. I already had Allen — it was hard enough learning to live with one male. Besides, I had it in my mind that I would be able to point out to this girl baby all the places I had gone wrong, and that would be at least one set of mistakes she wouldn't have to make. When I rode on the bus to work in downtown Cleveland and looked out the window at West Twenty-fifth Street, the way I'd been doing for years, when I washed the dishes staring at the yellow kitchen wall in front of me, when I waited in line at the bank or the supermarket, I'd be thinking of the things I'd have to tell her. About speaking up for yourself, about avoiding regret, how to tell if someone is lying, what to say when something is your fault.

And actually I was sure it would be a girl. I had only sisters, three of them, and I had the further evidence of other blood relatives: nine aunts to three uncles. My mother's mother raised her children by herself after Grandpa left — years of hard work and no rest, and then at last about ten years of sitting back and having the fruits of her labor: respect, tiny grandchildren to pet and hand back, meals being cooked for her in her own kitchen by her daughters and daughters-in-law. We are a family of bossy women, talky women, women who intend to be taken seriously. So it was natural that from my body, so like my mother's and my grandmother's, I would produce another woman. Allen had none of this sexual solidarity on his side. He had a brother and a sister, and no visible aunts or uncles. What could he say? He tried to get under my skin by bringing up rumors that twins ran in his family, but I took this for pure devilment.

We had an apartment then. What a trip it was, moving into that apartment. I remember how enamored I was of a green teapot — leaf green with gold trim. I put it up on a shelf over the sink and turned on the light nearby, to admire how it looked. That was the center of the apartment to me, that teapot on that shelf; it was the picture of what the rest of it would be when I fixed it up. It was night when we finished moving in and we all sat around and ate pizza — Annie from work, Allen's brother, John, and his buddy Ted; my best friend from school, Rose, and her sister Ellen; Jimmy Spicer and all that crew. All we had to drink was a six-pack of Champale that someone had brought and put in the refrigerator. No one would admit having brought it. We poured it into Dixie cups and drank it down, rank and beery-sweet.

Annie and Rose and I went to look at the bedrooms. Not Ellen — she wanted to stay with the guys: what a slut she was then. "This is going to be the baby's bedroom," I said to them. "It's going to be yellow and pink, two walls each color. Curtains with a yellow stripe." My old crib was in there already, scarred and scratched, wood-colored, pictures of lambs and rabbits at the head and foot. Probably we should have painted it, but I didn't want to cover up the lambs and rabbits — I'd looked at them, and so had my sisters, when we were too young to know what they were, and traced them with our fingers, and I wanted my girl to look at them with her unfocused eyes and pat them with her fat hands.

"Do you have a changing table?" Rose asked me. She didn't know a thing about changing tables and I knew it.

"No, and I don't want one," I said. "I'm going to use the top of the low dresser."

They looked at me, looked at my stomach, and looked away. They were horrified, I knew. I was horrified, too, in a way, by the swell of my stomach and by everything else, but also smug at having done it. Without even trying.

"Are you going to work after?" Annie asked me.

"When it's six months old, I'm going back." I was always very careful to say "it." I knew it was a girl but I felt it might jinx things if I said "she" right out. I was afraid something could shift in my body, a slow turn from one sex to the other.

"I don't think it's right to leave a little baby," Rose said. "Not until they go to school."

I sat down on a box and took my shoes off. "Give it a rest, Rose," I said. I knew she was saying what her mother said. They'd had no thought in their heads of babies, her and Annie. They weren't pregnant. They didn't know what to think of me at all. I leaned back against the wall and arched my spine, stretching, with the curve of my stomach pushed out. They looked at it, and their hands went to their own bodies. Annie put one hand on her stomach; Rose's fingers fluttered, touching her chest, her hips, twitching at her clothes.

"I'm going to breast-feed," I said.

"God, you're not," Annie said.

"I am, too," I said. "They get bigger if you do." All three of us looked at my chest.

This was bold talk on my part. Sometimes I felt quite different. Sometimes I wanted out of my body. I didn't feel bad, really—that wasn't it. I felt dreamy and sleepy. I sat for hours looking at baby books, reading about puréeing fruit and the order of immunization, sometimes sitting there looking out the window with my hand on the book, sometimes falling asleep with my cheek on the open pages. There was one book in particular that I liked, that said how to manage if you had one baby, then what to do if you had two, then three, then four. How to take four children for a trip on the bus was one of the things in this book. You were supposed to hold one by the hand who was holding another by the hand, one in a collapsible stroller, one in a sling against your chest. There was a picture of this woman wearing a dress and a hat, taking money out of her shoulder bag and giving it to the smiling bus driver, with all these round-faced children clustering around her like the angels that frame the margins of holy cards. I loved that book. I got it out of the library three times.

No, I felt fine, really. What worried me was this feeling of inevitability. I was going to have a baby and there was *nothing I could do about it.* I couldn't change my mind, couldn't say, "Wait, time out, I'd like to think about this for a minute." Somewhere in front of me were some solid hours of pain and a baby coming. I was going to grunt and bleed. My body was going to open. It was unbelievable, ridiculous, and yet I had to believe it.

I took the position of suspecting everything that was said to me. What did they know—"they" being the doctors and my female relatives? They were all so old. They'd been proved wrong already. I was proud I'd known I was pregnant before the doctor said so, even though the first two tests were negative. They'd said I'd have morning sickness, that I'd swell up with water, but I hadn't.

"What's the doctor doing for me?" I asked Allen. We were in bed and, against my protests, he was rubbing cocoa butter into my stomach, where the skin stretched over the baby. I wanted no special methods or precautions taken.

"What?" he said.

"Not a thing. Not a fucking thing."

He put his hand over my mouth. "Nice language for a mother."

I said I had to say it now, before I had to be a good example. I was feeling cross and cranky. I closed my eyes so as not to have to look at the greasy mound of my belly. I was seven-and-a-half months, and I finally needed to wear maternity clothes, instead of just unbuttoning the fly of my jeans and wearing a long shirt. My breasts were bigger already and Allen was showing signs of fascination with them, which I decided to find revolting and depraved.

"You have to go to the doctor," he said reasonably.

I hated him for saying this. "I go there and they make me give them a sample and the nurse weighs me and then I sit around in the waiting room with all these other swollen women and I read *Highlights* and then I go in and he gives me a hard time about gaining too much and asks if I've got any problems and I say no. That's it."

"Umhmm," Allen said. He moved his face against my shoulder, nuzzling from side to side, each side sweep carrying him a little farther onto my breast.

"Cut it out, Allen. Pay attention."

"Well, they can tell things from those tests, can't they?"

"You don't know anything about it. You don't know a thing." I threw the cocoa butter on the floor and rolled over.

It wasn't that I didn't want sex. Contrary to what the doctor had warned, I wanted it just as much as before. And I got a lot of attention, too, not only from Allen. I never would have credited it, but there are a lot of men who think it's sexy that you're pregnant. Even at nine months, when I was straining at the seams of these horrible maternity smocks, I got whistles when I was walking down the street. Guys would come up to me at parties and make jokes about buns in the oven, so as to have an excuse to pat my stomach. Partly it was curiosity, I'm sure. We'd never known anyone who got pregnant before — anyone our age, that is. I was the first in our crowd. Frankly, I looked great. My skin cleared up, for one thing.

So I wanted to do it. Allen wanted to do it. But when we did it, something was wrong. We seemed to be looking for each other, as if we were in a crowded room or a dark empty place; we knew the other person was there but we couldn't see each other. We kept trying, but it was no good. When we finished we'd hold each other, we'd turn on the radio and listen to late-night talk shows, and Allen would tell me jokes, and we'd fall asleep laughing. Some things were still okay.

But I worried about this full stop to the thrilling part of my sex life. Was this what had happened to all those sexless women my mother's age? You got pregnant and some switch in your body turned off all that teenage juice? You turned your cheek and pursed your lips instead of opening your mouth? You put your hands on his chest to push him away instead of to feel his hard little nipples? Watched TV together all evening, not talking, and then slept not touching?

By this time I'd cut my hours at the office to half, and all I had to do in the afternoons was sit around and think. How long does it take to do the dishes? I never made the bed. This is on principle: what's the point of making it look unused, unless it's to impress people? I could have baked but I was big as a house already. I could have watched the soaps. Actually, I did watch them sometimes, but half the actors and all the story lines were different from when I used to watch them in high school and I couldn't pay enough attention to catch up.

So I'd sit in the big armchair in the front room and look out the window and think. And I'd take long slow walks, thinking. Sometimes I thought about our honeymoon. It wasn't much, but it was fine. We went to Chicago, where we had friends we could stay with and save the cost of a motel, except one going and one coming back. With these friends, we went to some ball games and out dancing and hung out on the North Side the way we used to when we were all going to school there. At the time, I saw my adult life as a wonderful extension of my one year of college: lots of driving around, recreational drinking, and freedoms opening out one after another. The last day, we all went to the dunes on Lake Michigan with a picnic. We forgot the charcoal, but we were so hungry after swimming that we ate the hot dogs cold, with the warm wind blowing sand at us; grains of sand got between our teeth and made interesting gritty noises when we chewed. We grinned at each other, baring our sandy teeth, and we took pictures of our legs all lined up together, our pumped-up biceps, our arms buried from shoulder to wrist in sand, with only the hand sticking out, fingers wiggling. We all hugged each other after, and Allen and I drove off, still in our wet bathing suits, and immediately started looking for a motel, although it was only five-thirty. Even so, we didn't find one for a long time. Every NO VACANCY sign made us hotter. I sat as close to Allen as I could and tormented him while he drove, putting my hands inside his shirt and trying to undo his pants. A couple of times we pulled off the road and necked furiously, but we kept on. When we found a motel it was almost seven and we fell on each other, we melted for each other, we opened up all the way. That might have been the time, that one.

A month before my due date, supposedly spring, the weather was still gray, sleeting, dripping. I wasn't reading baby books anymore. All I had in front of me, between me and the baby coming, were a couple of "surprise" showers — one for my relatives, one for girlfriends. My mother had told me about them so I wouldn't turn up wearing something ratty. That was too bad. A surprise would have been distracting, at least — twenty dressed-up women hiding in closets and behind the living-room suite, jumping out. I sat around and felt sorry for myself for not having a surprise in my future.

Annie, Ellen, and Rose came over sometimes. I'd known them all since grade school, and they should have been a comfort. But I seemed to be looking at them from a long way off, across the great expanse of my stomach. I was so tired of it all, too tired to lift my hand or shake my head no when Annie brought me a cup of stinking herb tea. They sat and chattered about a whole fun world that was no longer open to me.

Shopping. I couldn't shop, couldn't bear to look at myself in a mirror. When I undressed at night I kept my eyes on a level so as not to see what was going on under my chin. Bad enough to see it with clothes over it. Going out for drinks after work. "Drinks," "work" — the words were no longer in my vocabulary. Sex, men, flirting: Ha. I wasn't a member of any sex anymore. I was a husk, a pod — a container, ready to split open.

I kept thinking and dreaming then of things coming open — of seams splitting, of cartons breaking and spilling their contents, of volcanoes, and, more horribly, of wounds, awful gashes that oozed unlikely substances: peanut butter, mud, ketchup. Sometimes it was melons slashed by a knife, all the seeds visible and gleaming wet. I could hardly stand to look at food just then, but I ate constantly, I just shoveled it in. Allen would watch me eat for another fifteen minutes after he'd finished—horrified, I think, to see all this stuff going in, maybe thinking I was going to explode, or give birth right there in front of him.

Allen was far away from me, too. Hugging was so ridiculous that I wouldn't let him do it. Kissing was out of the question, real kissing. To really kiss you have to wrap your arms around each other—neck, waist, wherever. You have to press up against each other, feel every part of his body pushing into or surrounding every part of yours. We lay in bed next to each other every night, holding hands, staring up at the ceiling until we fell asleep.

I stopped even thinking about the future. All there was, was now. There was my body with another body pushing around in it. I couldn't remember what my stomach, my breasts, had looked like before. I could hardly focus on the baby as any real thing. When Allen wanted to talk about names I really didn't care, but I made myself take a stand, on principle. There was no problem with a boy's name: Allen, for Allen; Joseph, for my father. We agreed about this, and, anyway, I still knew it would be a girl, and a girl had to be named this name I'd been carrying around since I was a kid, the name I'd wanted for myself instead of Bonnie: Rachel. It was not a silly name, not a name that could sprout a dopey nickname. It had a wonderful sound in your mouth. It was even biblical. But Allen wanted to name a girl after his sister. Debbie—I ask you. This is what we talked about those last weeks, constantly—at breakfast, at dinner, in bed. There was no compromise available, it seemed. We both hated all the other family names on both sides. We made lists. We read the *Best Baby Book of Names* to each other. It kept our minds off other things, like the fact that we were not allowed to screw anymore, even if we'd wanted to.

On a Saturday exactly two weeks before my due date, my mother-in-law drove over. Why? Who knows? Just to give us a hard time, is what I thought then. She came in and asked a lot of questions and poked around all over the apartment. Did I have my suitcase packed? Had I cooked up a lot of stuff and put it in the freezer for Allen to eat while I was in the hospital? Did I have a diaper service yet? The answer to all these questions was no. I could hardly bring myself to think about what was going to happen. I'd been telling myself there was plenty of time. It was just like when I was in school and there would be this big paper due that I had to do a lot of library research for, or I would have to make a clay relief model of South America with tiny products and resources glued to it. I would always start out with big plans, make lists, imagine the comprehensiveness of what it would be like when it was finished — the detail, the papier-mâché bananas, the small clay figures with miniature serapes. But I would put it off and put it off until there were only three days left, and then I'd panic for one day and rush around for another and stay up until two in the morning on the third, with my mother hovering anxiously over me as I grimly glued and pinned. So now the suitcase lay open and empty in our bedroom. The list of diaper services lay beside the telephone, unconsulted. I had no intention of freezing up big batches of lasagna or whatever.

"Allen wants to eat out while I'm gone," I said to my mother-in-law.

She was upset by this, I could see, but she had the good sense not to say anything.

To get out of the apartment, we went and got in the car and drove to the park near where we lived. It was real spring now, April, and actually warm. The sun was shining weakly. We parked and walked decorously down the path, the three of us. To our right there was a field with people playing catch and Frisbee, and some swings with children on them, swinging in great arcs, pointing their toes toward the sky. To our left there was the creek, and what Allen and I called the mountain. It was only a small hill, red clay and crumbling fast on its steep sides. But trees grew on it and there was a path on one side that you could scramble up to get to the top, which was a narrow ridge. Allen and I had often climbed it when we first lived in the apartment.

My mother-in-law was fussing with her purse as we walked. Allen had his hands in his pockets. He was scuffing up bits of leaves and gravel with the toes of his tennis shoes, walking his lively, good-natured walk. Even my mother-in-law, with her arthritic knees, was bouncing along. I felt like a sack of cement on stilts. What I wanted to do was climb the hill.

"Let's go up," I said to Allen.

"Don't be silly," my mother-in-law said.

"Come on, Allen," I said.

"You can't climb up there with that stomach," my mother-in-law said. She was showing alarm and I meanly enjoyed it.

"We can just go part way," I said to Allen, but I meant to go all the way once I got him up there.

He looked doubtful, but he followed me to the place where you have to step over the narrow arm of the creek that circles the hill. I stepped across, and stood waiting for him on the other side.

"Bonnie! Bonnie!" my mother-in-law called from the path. She was holding her purse in front of her with both hands.

"I'm going to do it!" I shouted to her.

We started up. The parts that were easy before were harder. The bits of the path where you had to plant your feet carefully because the ground sloped away were terrible. My balance was different. I felt like a tightrope walker, holding my arms out to keep upright. My stomach got in the way whenever I had to climb up and over the exposed roots of the trees, as if I were mounting a staircase. I had to scrabble up sideways and couldn't use my hands as much as I'd have liked. Finally we came to a part of the path that was like a chute, which you had to climb duckfooted, setting your feet at a careful angle, bending forward and rushing up, to use momentum. I did all that. Allen was just behind me. I made it up to the bend in the chute. I fell to my hands and knees.

"Bonnie! Bonnie!" my mother-in-law was yelling, and I could hear Allen gasping behind me.

"You dope, you jerk, you bitch," he said. He gripped me by my hips and shook them, put his arms around me, and pushed his face into the small of my back.

I let my arms relax until I was lying on my side, my face against the red crumbly clay, which was cool and slightly slick under my cheek. Looking up, I could see the top just above us, another ten feet — the hard ridge of the hill that I knew was bare of grass but carpeted with pine needles that slipped pleasantly under your feet. When you stood up at the top and looked down, the eroded sides, rawer and redder than the hard-packed soil of the ridge, sloped away from under your feet and you felt as if, with very little effort, you might slide down them into the water of the creek. Just one step, one small movement; no thought was necessary.

Allen was crying a little, which I thought was very sweet of him. "Oh, I'm all right," I said. I sat up so I could take his hand and kiss the palm. My mother-in-law was hesitating at the brink of the stepping-over place, holding her purse up almost over her head.

"I'm not going to do it!" I yelled to her.

"What?" she yelled back.

"I won't do it!" I yelled.

Allen and I started down. I slid down over the bad places on my butt, Allen going first to stop me if I fell. When we got to the bottom our clothes were dusty and smeared with red. My mother-in-law looked at us as if we were accident victims. "You'll be in the hospital before morning, after that," she said. I didn't care.

She was right, though. In the car on the way back I felt the first tightenings and loosenings, not yet pain. And after she'd gone home, I started to have mild contractions, and then a major one — the big pain rippling down, pushing my thoughts down, locating my center lower and lower. All the things I didn't know — when to start solid food, about Montessori, how to satisfy the sucking reflex — they didn't bother me a bit then, while I was going to the hospital with Allen in the car. It was like riding a comet or a roller coaster, this intense, purposeful movement after all those months of waiting. I didn't see anything ahead of me — not our lovely daughter; not the tired doctors who would talk to Allen afterward, my blood on their hands and their clothes; not my flattened, empty stomach; not my sallow face in the mirror the first time I could get up by myself and go to the bathroom; not Allen with a mask on his face bringing the baby through the door for me, with my lips saying "Rachel" for the first time. I didn't see any of that. But I could feel events rushing toward me as they wheeled me in. I could feel my life changing, the old familiar parts of it crumbling away and a new shape emerging that I would come to know, and, God, I was so excited I could hardly stand it.

Delphos, Ohio

CAMPBELL McGRATH

is where we turned around, surrendered to fate, gave in to defeat and
abandoned our journey at a town with three stoplights, one good mechanic
and a name of possibly oracular significance.

Which is how we came to consider calling the baby Delphos.

Which is why we never made it to Pennsylvania, never arrived to help J. B.
plant trees on the naked mountaintop he calls a farm, never hiked down the
brush-choked trail for groceries in the gnomic hamlet of Mann's Choice,
never hefted those truckloads of bundled bodies nor buried their delicate
rootling toes in the ice and mud of rocky meadows.

Blue spruce, black walnut, white pine, silver maple.

And that name! Mann's Choice. Finger of individual will poked in the face
of inexorable destiny.

Which is how we came to consider calling the baby Hamlet, Spruce or
Pennsylvania.

But we didn't make it there. Never even got to Lima or Bucyrus, let alone
Martin's Ferry, let alone West Virginia, let alone the Alleghenies tumbled
across the state line like the worn-out molars of a broken-down plow horse
munching grass in a hayfield along the slate grey Juniata.

Because the engine balked.

Because the shakes kicked in and grew like cornstalks hard as we tried to ignore them, as if we could push that battered blue Volvo across the wintry heart of the Midwest through sheer determination.

Which is foolish.

And the man in Delphos told us so.

Fuel injector, he says. Can't find even a sparkplug for foreign cars in these parts. Nearest dealer would be Toledo or Columbus, or down the road in Fort Wayne.

Which is Indiana. Which is going backwards.

Which is why they drive Fords in Ohio.

Which is how we came to consider calling the baby Edsel, Henry, Pinto or Sparks.

Which is why we spent the last short hour of evening lurching and vibrating back through those prosperous bean fields just waiting for spring to burst the green-shingled barns of Van Wert County.

Which is how we came to consider calling the baby Verna, Daisy, Persephone or Soy.

By this time we're back on the freeway, bypassing beautiful downtown Fort Wayne in favor of the rain forest at Exit 11, such is the cognomen of this illuminated Babel, this litany, this sculptural aviary for neon birds, these towering aluminum and tungsten weeds,

bright names raised up like burning irons to brand their sign upon the heavens.

Exxon, Burger King, Budgetel, Super 8.

Which is how we came to consider calling the baby Bob Evans.

Which is how we came to consider calling the baby Big Boy, Wendy, Long John Silver or Starvin' Marvin.

Which is how we came to salve our wounds by choosing a slightly better than average motel, and bringing in the Colonel to watch "Barnaby Jones" while Elizabeth passes out quick as you like

leaving me alone with my thoughts and reruns

in the oversized bed of an antiseptic room on an anonymous strip of indistinguishable modules among the unzoned outskirts of a small midwestern city named for the Indian killer Mad Anthony Wayne.

Which is why I'm awake at 4 A.M. as the first trucks sheet their thunder down toward the interstate.

Which is when I feel my unborn child kick and roll within the belly of its sleeping mother, three heartbeats in two bodies, two bodies in one blanket, one perfect and inviolable will like a flower preparing to burst into bloom,

and its aurora lights the edge of the window like nothing I've ever seen.

Eighteenth-Century Medical Illustration:
The Infant in Its Little Room

ANN TOWNSEND

Little sympathy, who kicks beneath my ribs
    for comfort, the clock reads 5:10
        and I am awake. Even held inside,

lightly under water, you hear everything
    and answer back to laughing voices, high music
        and the heartbeat, unceasing:

insistent baby, whose hands press out,
    who wakes me before light,
        the house is quiet except for us.

I don't know the moment I turned
    from one to two, when I began
        to think in plural. But long ago,

before sonograms and the x-ray's touch,
    before the Doppler monitor, one man drew
        what he thought was there, cupped inside

the cradle of the pelvis: another man,
    arms outstretched, a gold ring
        on each tiny finger.

Eyes raised, he looked
    for the place where music calls,
        where he might find a new world unfolding,

all glittering candlelight,
    graceful girls and bobbing flowers.
        Little one, we have this body

to ourselves, its ticks, its murmurs.
    We have a pulse, a subtle pressure.
        It drives us forward now, in time,

a late, insistent rhythm
    that plays as background
        for the waltz you've learned to dance.

Listening

DAVID MURA

for Samantha

And from that village, steaming with mist, riddled with rain,
from the fishermen in the bay hauling up nets of silver flecks;
from the droning of the Buddhist priest in the morning,

incense thickening his voice, a bit other-worldly, almost sickly;
from the oysters ripped from the sea bottom by half-naked women,
their skin darker than the bark in the woods, their lungs

as endless as some cave where a demon dwells
(soon their harvest will be split open by a blade, moist
meaty flesh, drenched in the smell of sea bracken, the tidal winds);

from the *torii* half way up the mountain
and the steps to the temple where the gong shimmers
with echoes of bright metallic sound;

from the waterfall streaming, hovering in the eye, and in illusion,
rising; from the cedars that have nothing to do with time;
from the small mud-cramped streets of rice shops and fish mongers;

from the pebbles on the riverbed, the aquamarine stream
floating pine-trunks, felled upstream
by men with *hachimaki* tied round their forehead

and grunts of *yoisho* I remember from my father in childhood;
from this mythical land of the empty sign and a thousand-thousand manners,
on the tip of this peninsula, far from Kyoto, the Shogun's palace,

in a house of *shoji* and clean cut pine, crawling onto a straw futon,
one of my ancestors laid his head as I do now on a woman's belly
and felt an imperceptible bump like the bow of a boat hitting a swell

and wondered how anything so tiny could cause such rocking unbroken joy.

This Night

CATHY SONG

Gently, you turn me over
so as not to wake
the baby sleeping in the fish
waters of my belly.
Swollen like a river
in the rainy season,
my hair straight and black
like our daughter's —
I am beautiful to you.
This I understand.
No longer the girl
who stood under the mango tree
half a lifetime ago,
my hair down to my knees,
but beautiful as mother of these
children whose beauty makes you weep
when you look at them
when they are fast asleep.
Salt of ocean,
salt of tears,
this you tell me,
sunlight harnessed in your arms.
Beautiful — mother of this
hovering in the midst of our desire.
You rub my feet,
bring me a glass of milk,
cold mango,
the color of hibiscus
honey clustered in moonlight.
This night outside the window.

Requiem

LIA PURPURA

to my child

Tap tap, like seconds piling, the robin stuffed quills of pine
    in the rafters, its beak plaited air, then *pock* in dry ground.
This was the morning measuring fear,
    the hours it took for the bird to make
of a cellophane wrapper a window, a floor,
    song in the shape of *safely graze*,
safe from hail, from sounds that sharpen in the grass
    and make the blades there real.
Of the same grass I walk easily over, that bird was working to
    stay above, stay above it, and sang of this work. I won't forget how
startling the moment it began, that low, breathy rumble
    when I turned the car on. How, driving off, I had no idea where
that lowest sound was issuing from — underneath, above, or trailing me?
    Of course it was. The insect sound
in the small space of the car, tape turning over,
    was somewhere, too, in the house this morning,
tap tap of finding the windowpane, more
    window than the wasp knew what to do with, dancing
along it, oddly dancing, a children's game, a child teasing:
    here, then gone. I was hearing all this, richest chords of
absence, entering the moving car, the children at play in the street near-
    missing and parting, each a map of wild intention,
and the morning held back in its history, black
    seed-sized eyes, vines-turned-thatching, ready
for lashing, bones hollowed for flight, songs rising,
    a shadow at its labor, lengthening

as the bird worked straight through outside my window.
    But I was not there to watch it all. I went out. We went: that fact
repeated down the day: we were driving out of town,
    and heavy as I was with you, daylight rose.
Deep inside I felt you turn, as a bird
    flew down to the highway's island
(oh the rushing storm we were in, the divided
    sea of cars in flight on either side of the dividing line),
and there in the pine, I slowed to see, was the bird's heavy breast
    more modest this time, with coloring enough
— of rusty copper, silty run-off — to please the eye, not enough
    for death to want yet, death stalking the yard as it does, with industry,
stalking the highway with speed, intimate as an eye
    brimming, as I was, and hauling, oh I was
tired then and you were running
    into your own beginning, that looping
hiss loose in the car, a conflagration, blast of sun
    the trucks unleashed behind them as they moved
ahead of us. And who was I, driving and pulling
    the sound of death along with me,
who saw day taking into its new body
    the light lampposts cast on the highway?
I could not watch the miles so staked
    nor make a game of counting and keeping
in this month before your coming,
    when every machine was grinding, adjusting,
or pushing through the terrible heat,
    terrible, for which the lesser heat of the car
made me grateful: for sanctuary: to be in a place
    that had not exploded: outside
the music: to have you in me.

You Have the Body

ELYSE GASCO

1

You meet your man at the outdoor market. He is standing in front of the fruits, feeling the melons and humming jazz. He stands there like the horn of plenty—gathering apples and plums, peaches and grapes, pressing them against his chest, holding them there with the strength of his chin. You pluck an apple from his neck and say: I am with child. He stares at you, not understanding, his mouth hanging open slightly like a little gash in his face. You wait for your words to wind their way through him, to wrap and curl into a knot of meaning. You are patient. You have nine months—give or take. Meanwhile, you snatch a few cherries and shove them slyly into your mouth. Your man's arms jerk out suddenly towards you—to embrace you or to push you away, it is all unclear—and the fruit tumbles to the ground. Things split apart. Seeds spill everywhere. The old vendor claps her hands in merriment but makes you pay for the fallen fruit anyway. At home you make a bruised-fruit salad and think up names to call the baby.

Selfish. This is how you feel. And you carry this selfishness around like a passport. Your borders, it seems, are already beginning to expand. Still, the world is vast and unsafe and feels as though it could end at any moment. Your friends tell you that there is no greater gift than the gift of life. They are puffy and romantic people, these friends of yours, and remember their childhoods with a boggy dreaminess that makes you wonder if you were ever actually young. Still, thinking about this gift, you wonder if a card wouldn't be just as nice, or maybe cash. Or maybe you should just give blood, something useful. Because once you give the gift, there is no returning it. It is, in fact, a final sale. And what will you say when this life falls apart, when the springs and doohickeys pop suddenly, pop right off, when the instruction manual frays and tatters, smudges and yellows. You suppose you could always tell this little life that in the end it is the thought that counts.

2

You use strange new words. You are surprised at how many times the word uterus comes up in conversation. And areola. And mother. When you say this word out loud you are surprised at how nasal you sound, as though you are joking or making fun of someone. It is common and then taunting and original. It seems self-explanatory, as though there is something in the sound of it that makes its relationship to everything self-evident, but for you the word has always needed a great deal of explanation. Your own mother, for instance, has never carried a baby to term. This seems impossible, really, as you stand there patting your flat belly with your open palm, for here you are. Surely, you must belong to her; the way you sleep with your arm flung across your eyes, the way you line the crisper of your refrigerator with paper towels and keep the mushrooms in paper bags, the way you clear the plates and begin the dishes even before everyone has finished eating. All these tidy things from your immaculate mother and yet how can she help you now?

You have another mother, one probably not quite as clean, who had an advertiser's uncanny imagination and ability to conceive of the whole thing from beginning to end, but for some reason just couldn't believe in it, just couldn't quite buy the product. What can you do? These mothers haunt you. You straddle these two women, somehow trying to keep your balance, a foot on each fragile back, reaching up like the top of a human pyramid. You have a sense that you are continuing something, but what it is that you are continuing is anybody's guess, like those strange games where you are asked to supply the noun, or verb or adjective, but you have no idea what the story is about, until it is read aloud to you in the end, and you realize how hysterical it is to have supplied all the inappropriate words. *Ladies and Gentlemen, please buckle your heads and place your lives in the upright position.* Things like that.

You want to be a part of a great generation of somethings, but it seems you are a kind of Eve, fiddling with your leafy underpants, lonely and nauseated, willing to pluck at anything for vitamins and reassurance. Really, you feel as though you are too curious for your own good, as though you are starting something up.

3

You are still flexible. You plié and bend your head towards your abdomen. You use your belly button as a megaphone and shout: Are you sure you want to go through with this? Eh? You wait for answers. You wait for signs. You think it should have a choice and you are willing to do whatever it wants. You do not feel at all like a mother; your elbows are still black and rough, you still get dirt underneath your fingernails. Instead, you feel more like a candidate. Your hands shake. You canvass your belly for votes of confidence. It is still too early to tell if you have a body of support.

You could almost forget. Its limbs are more like fins. The eyes are on the side of the head. Your imagination seems watery and strange. You take a lot of warm baths, your head submerged so that just your lips and nose break the surface, as though you were something feeding, and you listen to the sounds of fluid, the whoosh like blood through a vein. You imagine that you are the body of the one who could not keep you. She cannot stand the smell of steaming broccoli. She eats pomegranates, her fingers stained and messy from pulling at the seeds. She sleeps with anyone who asks her, trying to fight fire with fire. Absently, she kneads at her stomach, trying to flatten herself. At other times, you are your mother, and when no one is looking, you ease your fingers into yourself, looking for terrible blood.

Helpful people quote poetry at you. Everyone has something to say. At a dinner party with a Middle Eastern theme you fight to keep your tabouli down. When you refuse a glass of wine, a man with hummus in his moustache recites Kahlil Gibran. You have heard this one before. *Your children are not your children / They are the sons and daughters of Life's longing for itself.* Now you say it so often it becomes like a riddle or a joke. You ask: When are your children not your children? And your man answers: When they are the sons and daughters of life's longing for itself. After a while, like all the best lessons in life, like all the finest words, if you say them too often, if you say them too fast, they begin to make no sense.

Your man is very *que sera*. You can hear him humming to himself: Whatever will be, will be. For some reason though, he has stopped shaving. His beard grows erratically across his face, lurching across his cheeks in fits and starts, leaving small patches of stubbly clear-cut in odd places. You have never seen him quite so hairy and you wonder what he is trying to do. When you sleep beside him at night it feels as though he is incognito. He breathes like a spy, like someone waiting behind a door. You have never felt more alone and you cannot figure out your relationship to anything. Sometimes, when he reaches for you at night, you feel as though you are lying under an assumed name.

This is how you imagine it—when your child takes over the house and holds itself hostage in a bedroom. There you are, standing in front of a closed door, afraid to knock again. Inside, all will be quiet and still, and it will remind you of a different time, a time when the door was softer but just as impenetrable. Whatever is happening in there is happening without you. Every now and then you will hear a gasp and it will shoot through you like a torpedo, like a fist through your heart. And you too will gasp, in reflex, in pure jerky pain. You will stand at the door whispering secret words like a game-show host. You will say: Honey? Sugar? Sweetie pie? And the voice from the room will answer: Things made with glucose. You will laugh and feel relieved. You would throw a pie in your face for this kid. But when you knock again, a voice hits the wood of the door like spit. Go away, it says. And you will want to ask: Where? You will want to ask directions in a world where maps are useless and imprecise. The signs for the distance between each place are all way off.

You are haunted by her in her new breezy body, walking somewhere, let's say, through a green park or a field of some tall prickly flowers. Her irresponsible little hips swishing, she moves with the smug jauntiness of a remorseless litterbug. There is no word for the kind of criminal she is; a crook who leaves things behind. Something messy billows behind her. "Hey," you want to shout, grouchy like a park attendant spearing the ground, picking up garbage. "Hey, you can't just leave that there."

People tell you that now you will be complete. This makes you wonder what they thought of you before. Incomplete, obviously. An unfinished course, hanging somewhere between passing and failure. It is true that often you feel as though you are missing some essential elements, some crucial parts. "Let's face it," says a girl you have only pretended to like, your man's ex-lover, who is eccentric enough to still be his friend and is regarded as well developed. "Before this, you were pretty childish." "I was?" you ask. And for some reason you want to stick your fingers in your nose. Everyone smells. Some seem to be smugly taking bets on what kind of a mother you will be. You are drawn to these grumps. You peer over their shoulders looking for a tip, trying to figure out what the odds are. You begin to count the number of times someone says to you: I just can't imagine you as a . . . well anyway. Still others are even less fun. They are blunt but mysterious. They say simply: Into this world? Aghast, as though they knew another, better, place and if you waited long enough they might reveal this choice travel destination, this exclusive sunshine spot. For fun, you divide these friends of yours into two groups. Those who pronounce fertile so that it rhymes with servile. And those who say it just like turtle. You appreciate the latter. These people seem to have a sense of humour. And you have a strong affinity for this slow reptile; its horny toothless beak, and its soft, stout body enclosed within a shell.

You wake your man in the middle of the night. You say: Quick. When are your children not your children? He is not easy to wake up. He grinds his teeth as though he is chewing something and you can tell that in the future you will be up many nights alone. He mumbles something strange and garbled. You hear: Slums and slaughters. You are losing the poem. Like you, it is growing slippery and changing shape. You lie there getting the words wrong, trying to make sense. Everything seems to be on the tip of your tongue and maybe that is why you cannot speak. You think: They are the slums and slaughters of life's lunging for your neck. They are the guns and plotters. They are the sins and robbers. They will steal your heart away.

It is not at all like having a cat. Your cat is always your cat; there aren't many changes in this relationship. You both might vary your favourite resting spots, your desires for certain foods might wax and wane, but still it is all one long continuum, neither of you ever really interrupting each other, few surprises — old age, death. That kind of thing. Plus, he is neutered. This is something completely different. You could be blamed. In your dreams you are given a choice. You can be Mary, Mother of God, or you can be Dr. Frankenstein. Select now.

Lying with the cat across your stomach, this is what you imagine: you will give the son a Barbie doll. You will try to introduce him to his feminine side. It will be an awkward first meeting. But hopefully soon he will develop and sprout like a proper theory. With loopholes. Because eventually you will have to let him out of the house. Like tropism, he will bend and grow towards the light of the outside, which at times can look eerily like the glow of the television set. He will come home, aim Barbie at your head and say: Pow-pow, mommy. One day you will catch him prying open the legs of the doll, saying: C'mon. Show Ken what you got, hon. What will you do? You will do the best you can. You will teach him about foreplay. You will put condoms in his lunch pail, hidden between the Twinkies and the trail mix.

5

What can you say about your man, except that you are no longer sure that you trust him. He smells like that strange papaya shampoo. He cooks things in the kitchen, shrimps and weird sauces that he knows you can't eat, that make you gag. Sometimes when he lies in front of the television, his mouth hanging open a little, his shirt unbuttoned to his waist, you think: God Almighty, I have made a tragic mistake. I have mated badly. Shouldn't he be preening? Shouldn't he be trying to impress you, carrying sharp twigs in his mouth, swinging from the tallest tree, patting down the earth, stomping and bellowing, ready to protect you from anything? You have always been torn between love and solitude and you think that now you might be crowding yourself right out of your life. When he persists in asking you what you want to eat, you wonder how he ever got into your house. Just what part does he think he actually played in this whole thing? Sometimes when he sees you reach into your pants fearfully checking for drops of blood, he takes it as a sign of lust. You are so wrapped up in your biology it is difficult to understand just what it is that he is doing. Lying underneath him, your whole body groping towards some unimaginable destiny, you say: You know, there is a vas deferens between us. But he does not understand himself enough to get it.

You are surprised when the doctor says that everything is progressing normally. You do not think that you have a history of progressing normally. In your medical file under Family History you have a lot of question marks. You do not know your disease ancestry. You do not know how your mother's labour went, except that here you are. The nurse gives you a few pamphlets to take home and read, brochures, you like to call them, flashy and colourful, like something you might get at a car dealership for something you should decide on with a test drive. Inside one of them you read: *Now you might become curious about your own mother's pregnancies and deliveries.* And you think that this is true. You might.

You imagine her alone. What did this woman know about love anyway? She wore her jeans until they bulged. She drank in dark bars and fell over into the laps of strangers. One night she went home with a piano player and she didn't even wince when he squeezed her swollen breasts. She was flippant with her proteins, fast and loose with her calcium supplements. It's a wonder you are even alive. Is it possible to fill every second of the day so that you never have a moment to think? Once, your mother told you, "I seem to remember something about her being a nurse." A nurse? A fluffy do-gooder student with a fat ponytail and a delicate bedpan manner—gone bad. A defeated caregiver who failed at nursing, whose uniform pulled and gaped in disgrace, whose ankles swelled in her thick white shoes. A crazy woman in her protective mask, switching around the babies in the nursery. Maybe she loved a doctor, an orderly, a patient who died. Maybe some heartless resident promised her a house in the country and then left her for a cardiologist. Your mother sends you recipes in the mail for high-protein shakes, and an article about soya beans. She highlights all the important food groups and suggests fresh ginger for nausea and it is then you realize that she has always known how to take care of you.

You go for your first ultrasound. In the hospital you find yourself staring at the nurses. Most of them wear glasses and seem withdrawn. When the technician rolls the probe across your stomach you realize that you are watching her instead of the screen. This is a habit you picked up from contemplating the stewardesses on airplanes, convinced that they will be the first to register signs of impending danger, disaster. Who knows what you are making in there, what strange materials you are actually made of. You wait for the technician's facial expressions to change, but she just seems bored. She does not seem like a good caregiver. She begins to read out the parts like a merchandise list. Finally, you glance at the screen and there it is, unbelievably yawning and raising a small hand in a kind of salute. Your man grabs your hand in a sudden rush of disbelief and implication. Oh, the things that grow out of the murkiest longings. The technician asks if you have any questions. You say: Ask if it wants to be born. Finally the woman laughs a little and says: Everything wants to be born. It is the urge to life. Really? you say. Because you desperately want to believe this person who has pronounced your centre alive and well, and you have always had such a hard time summoning up your own eagerness, your own importunity. You are possessed by a strange knowledge, like the realization that most of the dust in your house is actually your own skin. Everywhere you go you leave pieces of yourself. This is an awesome responsibility. You want so badly to believe in the impulse to life, but you remember high school, the horror of those young, urgent lives, grown-up and edgy, and suddenly you feel sick and guilty.

How could you not have noticed before all the pregnant women, all the children on the street, all products of a mounting desire, however brief, however fleeting. You are like someone back from the moon, bewildered by station wagons and family vans, by car pools and video games. What does any of that have to do with what you just saw? You and your man walk home like the first people on earth. You want to take off your shoes and go barefoot. You want to lie face down in the soil somewhere, to smell something real, to plant yourself and grow bushy and full of yourself, like human nature. How can you not feel like a kind of Eve? How can you not want to know everything?

When your child is at school you will memorize encyclopedias. You will read the Trivial Pursuit cards in the bathroom. You will keep the *Book of Lists* under your mattress like an erotic magazine. You will blush with useless knowledge. Secretly you will relearn how to multiply fractions. At dinner one night you might be feeling particularly confident. You will risk everything then. You will say: Go ahead. Ask me anything. I dare you. And your daughter will reach into her chest, pull out her heart and spread it across the table like a royal flush. She will murmur: Look. Who are you? Why does it hurt? All this will stun and frighten you and so you will tell her that the Virginian opossum has as many as seventeen teats. You will tell her that Julius Robert Oppenheimer's main aim was the peaceful use of nuclear power. You will tell her that the atmosphere not only provides us with oxygen, it also protects us from the sun's harmful radiation and the excesses of cold and heat. You will tell her that some people think aliens built Stonehenge. And you will remind her that the peculiar thing about fractions is that when you multiply them, no matter how fruitfully and with what attention, you always end up with less than you expected.

6

Your mother sends you a baby picture of yourself at three weeks, your head still a little misshapen from the inside of some other woman's body, the tremblings of her faithless muscles. You have never been all that gentle with yourself, but for the first time you want to reach out, pick yourself up, and stroke your splotchy newborn forehead. You have a hard time giving anything away, even an old pair of shoes. Spiders rule your bathroom. When a plant dies you never really know what to do with its body, its dusty and crackled-earthy remains. When a cat followed you home, ugly with an eye infection, you cried, but you kept him. Your mother writes that you should send her pictures of yourself, of your ampleness, your unfurling belly button like a pig's nose. But you are embarrassed. Not only by your plain and palpable lust, but by something even more unexpected—your natural and painless fecundity. "I am fecund," you say to your mirrored reflection, and you feel suddenly dangerous and gritty, as though somehow the very term has all the innuendos of a dirty word. You cannot send this image of yourself to your mother, in the bulging costume of a braggart, the grotesque adornment of a betrayer. A strange riddle twists through you with the power and intention of a snake. When is your mother not your mother?

You watch a television show about population growth. A science-fiction writer gloomily suggests that women should just stop having babies for a while, to give the earth time to heal and repair. He says you have to be careful. He says that soon there will be no more room left on the planet. He says we will all die of thirst or claustrophobia. You are so easy to blame. Your shirts do not button properly. You are slow and often dreamy. You whistle for no reason and cry unexpectedly. The TV flashes pictures of dying children, of orphans waiting to be adopted, their legs skinny and bowed, their tiny ribs like washboards. And you think: Oh, pretty please. Just this one. There must be just a little space for this one. Still, you cannot know what you are about to set free and unmuzzled into this world.

7

Spring comes early. Birds lean up against your window like buskers, like colourful folk singers whistling through the screen. It is not strange to you at all that you have timed it to the month of your own birth. You think of life and all its repeating demands. How could anyone have ever thought the world was flat? It is so obviously round, circling over and over again. All the movements inside remind you of live fish held in a plastic bag, creatures you could fool yourself into thinking required the minimal amount of care. Sometimes you imagine that it cannot breathe, that you yourself are made of plastic, artificial and smothering. For both of you there is finally only one way out. You picture the way you must have bruised her inside, or lodged a heel right under a rib, or pressed yourself hard into her bladder or a kidney, forcing her to remember you there. You waited with her like a prisoner, though it is difficult to tell just who was holding who hostage. Clearly she must have gotten the poem wrong, misheard it somehow in a very crowded room so that she could have turned to you and said in all seriousness, in the voice of a poet: Don't you know you are not my child?

8

You are heavy and at times this feels only indulgent. Everyone can see what you are up to. Standing, stretching, anything erect, really, is not as much fun as it used to be. All you want to do is squat. Life moves vigorously now and sometimes when you look down at yourself you can see your own shirt actually moving, fleeting jabs and undulations. When this happens in public you feel like a suspect, a shoplifter, someone whose thievery and hunger is so painfully obvious.

Lately you cannot imagine being loved. You do not know what you will ever do to deserve it. You stay up late eating cheese popcorn and watching terrible movies. Every night it seems there is something on about the invasion of aliens, rubbery things looking for a new home, lodging in people's faces or taking over their lawn mowers. You watch these sad, awful creatures covered in phlegm or mucous as though they've been crying way too long, battling all of life, and you think: Let them be sons and daughters. Let them be songs and drifters. Just let them be. It seems you cannot stop checking the clock or flipping through the pages of your datebook. Suddenly it feels as though you have run out of time to change the world. You decide that if the one inside you needs to burrow into some part of your face or to take over a favorite appliance, you will let it. When you do finally fall asleep, this is what you dream:

One day the child will wake up with a strange glint in the eye, a tiny grimace like a smudge in the crook of the mouth. But when you lick your finger and go to wipe it off, it will be indelible. The child will watch you suspiciously, the way you watch someone blowing up a balloon — waiting for the bust. The child will stalk you warily around the house, and the look will remind you of a time when people used to pick up your hand and say in amazement, "Look at this tiny wrist. I could break it like that." In the child's eyes is a strange brew of disgust and pity and you will see that this child is afraid of becoming you. The child will develop a cruel interest in your life, following you around the house like the paparazzi, asking cunning and subtle questions like: "At what point exactly do you think your life went wrong?" And: "When did you finally let go of your dreams to settle for this?" And you will know that there is no such thing as planned parenthood. All the things you will do right will be by mistake.

In the last weeks you imagine that there is another choice. You are as cranky and unpredictable as a cat. You just want to go off somewhere alone. You know it isn't his fault, but lately when you look at your man, just the sight of him makes you feel like complaining. You imagine that you would be better off on your own where nothing horrible could come out of your mouth. He cannot get his arms around you any more and it feels as though the sheer size of you is already pushing him away. Is it ever possible to get close without really contorting? When he sleeps, peaceful and oblivious, you watch him and think: Idiotic. Nightly, you plan your escape. Two steps to the bedroom door. Twenty-one steps down the hall to the front door. You see yourself behind the wheel of your car, the windows wide open, your hair tangling into thick clumps. Suddenly, the whole world is there, waiting. What do you want? Ocean? Desert? The cold, dark mountains? The road ahead is flat and inviting. Soon, you will be skinny again. You will only wear dresses. You will never be afraid of strangers. You will drink men under the table and sleep with college freshmen. They will read to you excitedly from their textbooks, their cheeks still raw from shaving too fast. You will take a woman lover and live in North Africa with a turban wrapped around your head. There are many sleepless nights like these and you watch your room getting lighter, like tanned skin being peeled back to reveal the pale below. You think that this is like death in the way it makes you want to tidy, to put your affairs in order. You remember all the boys you've slept with and rate them one to ten. Could this really be the last one? You rub your stomach, gently poking at the tiny heel you feel pressing just below your ribs and you wonder: Whose body are we?

9

It happens in a rage. In the beginning it does not seem quite so overwhelming, and you are overcome by shyness. A nurse, her hair pulled back into a tight braid, takes your blood pressure. She smells like rubbing alcohol and peppermint gum and you try to win her over by controlling your facial expressions. Maybe, with enough effort, you will appear neutral and serene. Maybe you can keep all your grunts and animal belling to yourself. You want to show her that you will be no trouble at all. You say: Maybe I could just do this with my underwear on? She gives you a world-weary smile and pats your hand. Her nails are short and clean and filed square. In the end, though, there is nothing demure about life. Instead you find that you have ripped the hospital gown from your body. Your man seems amused but beaten and you cannot bear for him to touch you. Later he will tell you that all you kept shouting was *out*, but he could not believe that you were actually talking to him. You stare into the eyes of the nurse beside you. She seems strong and encouraging. This thing is a battle and until now, you could not conceive of how much you must have hurt her, the scars you left on the woman who left you behind. When they deliver the small blue girl onto your stomach, you are amazed that something so tiny could be so resolute, so earnest. They lift her to you and for one moment you imagine not taking her in your arms, closing your eyes, politely refusing her as though she were a festive party offering, a decadent loot bag or a fancy canapé you might politely decline with a simple *No thank you. Not tonight. Watching my weight. Oh, I couldn't possibly.* Her eyes are a liquid steel colour and she holds your stare easily while you trace her stringy veins with your fingertips; your powerful blood, her iron will. It seems this child will never not be your child. Whatever were you thinking? It is impossible to be this other woman's exhausted body now, her damp sad belly, her sticky hair, her dry bitten lips. They tag your daughter's wrist and you will follow her forever like a wildlife biologist. You hope that someday she will learn to forgive you.

The nurse squeezes your shoulder and quickly turns to leave. She will not turn around again, and you see that she is the one with the braid and that it is coming undone in what seems to you like a kind of abandonment, held together by just a plain rubber elastic. She has left the baby swaddled beside you in the crook of your arm, in your lawless hands that would steal anything for this girl. The nurse makes a sound, a laugh, a tired sigh, something breathy, and pushes the door open with her strong shoulder. She is leaving you alone with this child. She does not tell you that she will be back. Her white coat billows a little like the sail of a small boat surprised by the wind—goodbye, goodbye. You watch her leave and wonder: Wait. Where are you going?

Notes from the
Delivery Room

My Mother Gives Birth

JULIANNA BAGGOTT

They gave her a form of truth serum,
not to dull the pain, to dull memory.
But she does remember
asking the nurse to take off her girdle —
not a girdle but her skin taut with pain —
that the nurse told her to stop screaming,
the girl one over was having her first
and scared enough already.
She rolled my mother to her side, standard procedure,
handcuffed her to the bed rails, left her to labor alone.
My mother says her last thought was of Houdini,
that she too could fold the bones of her hands
and escape. I want her to slip free,
to rise up from her bed and totter
out of that dark ward of moaning women.
I want to be born in black dirt.
But her mind went white as cream lidding a cup.
And she does not remember,
although her eyes were open, blank,
how I spun from her body, wailing,
drugged for truth, my wrists on fire.

Transition

TOI DERRICOTTE

the meat rolls up and moans on the damp table.
my body is a piece of cotton over another
woman's body. some other woman, all muscle and nerve, is
tearing apart and opening under me.

i move with her like skin, not able to do anything else,
i am just watching her, not able to believe what her
body can do, what it *will* do, to get this thing accomplished.

this muscle of a lady, this crazy ocean in my teacup.
she moves the pillars of the sky. i am stretched into
fragments, tissue paper thin. the light shines through
to her goatness, her blood-thick heart that thuds like
one drum in the universe emptying its stars.

she is
that heart
larger
than my life
stuffed
in
me
like sausage
black sky
bird
pecking
at the bloody
ligament

trying
to get
in, get
out
i am

holding out with
everything i
have
holding out
the evil thing

when i see there is
no answer
to the screamed
word
GOD
nothing i can do,
no use,

i have to let her in,
open the door,
put down the mat
welcome her
as if she
might be the
called for death,
the final
abstraction.

she comes
like a tunnel
fast
coming into
blackness
with my headlights
off

     you can push . . .

i hung there. still hurting, not knowing what to do.
if you push too early, it hurts more. i called the
doctor back again. *are you sure i can push? are you sure?*

i couldn't believe that pain was over, that the punishment was enough, that the wave, the huge blue mind i
was living inside, was receding. i had forgotten there
ever was a life without pain, a moment when pain wasn't
absolute as air.

why weren't the nurses and doctors rushing toward me?
why weren't they wrapping me in white? white for respect,
white for triumph, white for the white light i was being
accepted into after death? why was it so simple as saying
you can push? why were they walking away from me into
other rooms as if this were not the end the beginning of
something which the world should watch?

i felt something pulling me inside, a soft call, but i
could feel her power. something inside me i could go
with, wide and deep and wonderful. the more i gave
to her, the more she answered me. i held this conversation
in myself like a love that never stops. i pushed toward
her, she came toward me, gently, softly, sucking like a
wave. i pushed deeper and she swelled wider, darker when
she saw i wasn't afraid. then i saw the darker glory
of her under me.

why wasn't the room bursting with lilies? why was
everything the same with them moving so slowly as if
they were drugged? why were they acting the same when,
suddenly, everything had changed?

we were through with pain, would never suffer in our
lives again. put pain down like a rag, unzipper skin,
step out of our dead bodies, and leave them on the
floor. glorious spirits were rising, blanched with
light, like thirsty women shining with their thirst.

i felt myself rise up with all the dead, climb out of
the tomb like christ, holy and wise, transfigured with
the knowledge of the tomb inside my brain, holding the
gold key to the dark stamped inside my genes, never to
be forgotten . . .

it was time. it was really time. this baby would be
born. it would really happen. this wasn't just a
trick to leave me in hell forever. like all the other
babies, babies of women lined up in rooms along the halls,
semi-conscious, moaning, breathing, alone with or without
husbands, there was a natural end to it that i was going
to live to see! soon i would believe in something larger
than pain, a purpose and an end. i had lived through to
another mind, a total revolution of the stars, and had
come out on the other side!

one can only imagine the shifting of the universe, the
layers of shale and rock and sky torturing against each
other, the tension, the sudden letting go. the pivot of
one woman stuck in the socket, flesh and bones giving
way, the v-groin locked, vise thigh, and the sudden
release when everything comes to rest on new pillars.

where is the woman who left home one night at 10 P.M.
while everyone was watching the mitch miller xmas show?
lost to you, to herself, to everyone

they finished watching the news, went to sleep,
dreamed, woke up, pissed, brushed their teeth, ate
corn flakes, combed their hair, and on the way out
of the door, they got a phone call . . .

while they slept the whole universe had changed.

from *Still Life*

A. S. BYATT

They put her in a bare room with a white bed, a bedside table, a chair, a carafe, and a very small white canvas sling on tubular metal struts, which she only slowly understood, as she climbed docile onto that new bed, to be a cot. And it was only when she saw that small cot that she understood for the first time what was happening—that this was not an ordeal that had gripped her to test her, that two people were here. That this was happening to two people. That someone had to get out. That it was inconceivable that the female body could ever be open or elastic enough to allow anything the size of a baby to come out. That nevertheless there must be an end—it *must* . . . The nurses were about to leave her alone in this room. She said with the first agitation she had shown that she must have her books; they must bring her books. Books? they said.

"In the suitcase."

"They don't bring suitcases to the delivery rooms."

"*I must have my books.*"

"We'll see . . . when anyone has time . . . We're very busy . . . four mums came in at once; we're off our feet. Which book do you want, then?"

"All my books. How do I know. The Wordsworth. All of them. Particularly Wordsworth."

"Wordsworth?"

"Poems. If you've time."

"Wordsworth's poems." The green nurse seemed blank. "I'll do what I can," she said, placating.

"How long?" said Stephanie.

"I couldn't say. You're doing fine. First babies always take longer. Try and relax."

They left her alone. To try and relax. With a bulbous bell push on a long furry flex depending from the ceiling, no instructions about when she would need to ring it and when, as the English require, she must be silent and uncom-

61

plaining. At first she lay dutifully and stared at the white ceiling, slowly turning her head to take in the fact that it was an unusually sunny day, that small, shining white clouds, light rimmed, were being blown across a blue sky, that she was on the ground floor with a part-open window that looked onto a closed courtyard of grass. She no longer had her watch, which had gone with her clothes; she thought it must be mid-morning, even midday, but was not sure. She thought for the first time of Daniel. She had not told Daniel she was here. This was because of Mrs. Orton and Marcus, who between them prevented any normal converse at all. It ought to have been possible to rely on those two to tell Daniel, but it was not. She began to worry, and then the pain took over. There was something ridiculous about lying there on one's back while it pulled — and something unnecessarily painful. She rolled sideways with effort, inducing rippling cramps. She wished she had Wordsworth. She swung her legs off the bed, in the next lucid interval, and walked to the window. The air was cold and clear and amazingly fragrant. She peered out. All around the wall, under the windows, were wallflowers — small, velvet-brown, straw-gold, rust-colored shabby flowers, and their warm, generous smell moved on the air. She breathed, holding the window frame, and then, obeying some powerful instinct, began to march up and down the room rhythmically, turning on her heel at the walls, head up, nostrils flared. The next pain, when it came, was possible to weave into the rhythm of this tramping, to time between wall and wall and back again. She began to observe it almost from outside, listening to its rise and fall, letting it make its way. The adrenaline, lost with the enema, flooded back. She tried to recall the "Immortality Ode," which was yet another rhythm. The Rainbow comes and goes. And lovely is the Rose. She strode on. When they opened the door she did not immediately stop, and then came to a halt, conscious of their eyes on her flapping gown and naked buttocks.

"Get back into bed, please, dear, now. You shouldn't be out of bed."

"It's easier, walking."

"You'll make it harder for yourself, using your energy up. You'll contract your muscles. Try and relax. Come on now."

"Look. If I use *these* muscles, I relax *those* . . . It hurts less."

"Don't be silly, dear. Get back into bed like a good girl."

She stood stupidly, and the pain choked again like a suffocating net, as it did when they interfered with its liveliness, so that she swayed, and had to be helped to the bed, where they listened again with their silver funnel, put their hands inside her and made notes, while she smiled politely and the pain rustled jagged and uncomfortable and died away. They timed this meager contraction wisely, told her she'd a long time to go, and prepared to leave again. If she felt she needed to bear down, they said, she was to ring.

She had no idea what this need might feel like, or how easy it might be to identify. It was somehow not possible to ask. She did ask if she could have Wordsworth and her watch and was answered as before: they were short staffed, they would try, she was to be good. When they were gone she had lost her sense of her own rhythms, wanted desperately to get out and walk again and yet was afraid of being reprimanded for being a naughty girl. And she had forgotten, or not been given time, to mention Daniel. After thought, she got up on her hands and knees, moaning softly, swaying from side to side. The pain resumed its clear, relentless pattern, and she worked with it, hot and tiring. No doctor had come. She supposed that was all right. The pain gripped like a claw. The day wore on, and she rocked, and then, since no one came, walked some more, breathing very hard. Through the window with the warm sweet flower smell came the sound of someone screaming regularly and on a rising pitch. Stephanie heard herself thinking that it would be helpful, but not English, not good manners, to make a noise like that.

The desire to "bear down," when it came, proved to be unlike any sensation she had experienced, and immediately recognizable for what it was. It had the appalling, uncontrollable nature of severe diarrhea pains but was otherwise different, in that nothing knotted. Something heavy and hard and huge inside her opened her out like a battering ram and the pain was no longer defined and separate from her but total, grasping, heating, bursting the whole of her, head, chest, wrought and pounded belly, so that animal sounds broke from it, grunts, incoherent, grinding clamor, panting sighs. She managed to roll herself back onto the bed, during this, and clutch the pear-shaped bell. Her vision filled with nasturtium pale scarlet, and then with a curtain of blood. The purple nurse returned. Stephanie moaned wildly that it was coming back; the pain, like an incoming tide, abated a little, rippled back, gathered itself and sprang, *heavy*.

She was a woman who had thought about the ambivalence of female imagining of internal spaces. The moon, whatever we believe about its real size, appears to us to be a silver disk about a foot across and two miles distant. The womb, imagined, can appear to be a tiny crumpled purse to hold half a crown, or silent underground caverns, receding endlessly, corrugated, velvet, blood dark, gentian dark. Blood before it meets the air is blue. And the vagina, which grips a tampon securely, which admits a man who can, a large man like Daniel, blindly explore the lost and charged tip of its cul-de-sac, a pocketed shaft with elastic muscles — how can that narrow sheath take a furious blunt block that appears to the perception of inner spaces to be larger than the body itself, to be breaking out as it expands and can no longer be contained? The spine, Stephanie's shrinking mind stated, is a plane, *flat* on the bed, as though by butchery the belly is severed and the flanks fall. Beneath the helpless trunk a whole wall, a box-side of flesh and cracking bone seemed to rear and expand between the bursting thing and the air. There were now two nurses, holding the legs up, peering under. Some relief could be found by moving the feet rapidly in circles, but one nurse slapped these and reiterated the admonition about not contracting muscles. She was amazed at the rage she felt. She wished the woman dead for holding her so uncomfortably in an unnatural position. Her head thrashed from side to side. The thing launched itself again against its prison walls and she thought of time. How long was this to last? As long as the walking and singing? She had been wrong. It could *not* be endured. It rose and drove and the brain throbbed and banged, and from somewhere, even as they cried hold back, don't push, she found the desperate energy to end the pain by increasing it, to *tear through* the flesh wall, and cried out, loud, groaning, defeated, as the body split in half and on her soaked thigh she felt, incredulous, a warm wet ball, with its own fluttering pulse, not hers.

Hold back, they said, more urgently, and she found she now could. Silence flooded back after the bloodstorm; at the stretched entrance they turned small shoulders with careful hands. Push now, they said, and the muscles dictated mildly, push; and the thing slid away, compact, solid, rubbery, trailing, gone. She could see nothing, only feel their hands busy, far away. And then a voice gasped, choked, thin and scratching, and then with a note in it wailed, on a repeated, climbing catch. "A lovely boy," said the purple nurse. "A lovely big boy." The green nurse was pressing the suddenly diminished hump; *push*, she said, and as the rhythm died, the body pushed for the last time and Stephanie heard the liquid slither of the afterbirth. The boy wailed again, and the woman saw, beyond her feet and the stained sheets, the purple nurse carrying the small blood-red body compact on one hand. She closed her eyes and lay back, solitary, surprised to be solitary, to hear the beat of her own life only, after so long.

They brought the boy to her, his small neck and lolling head coming turtle-like out of a hospital gown like her own in miniature. It was not a time, or a hospital, where the child is put immediately to the mother's breast. But, for a space of time, he lay beside her on the pillow and she raised herself a little and looked sideways and down, damp and exhausted.

She had not expected ecstasy. She noted that he was both much more solid, and, in the feebleness of his fluttering movements of lip and cheek muscle, the dangerous lolling of his uncontrolled head, more fragile, than she had expected. His flesh was dark and mottled, and creamy wax and threads of blood clung here and there. Pasted to his pointed head, its overlapping cap of bone already springing apart under the elastic scalp, was a mat of thick black hair. He had a square brow, Daniel's brow, tiny nostrils, and a creased, emphatically large mouth. A clenched fist, smaller than a walnut, brushed a finely curled ear. He bore little, but not no, relation to the furious thing that had breached her. As she looked he frowned, increasing his look of Daniel, and then, as though aware of her gaze, opened ink-blue eyes and stared at her, through her, past her. She put out a finger and touched the fist; he obeyed a primitive instinct and curled the tiny fingers round her own, where they clutched, loosened, tightened again. "There," she said to him, and he looked, and the light poured through the window, brighter and brighter, and his eyes saw it, and hers, and she was aware of bliss, a word she didn't like, but the only one. There was her body, quiet, used, resting; there was her mind, free, clear, shining; there was the boy and his eyes, seeing what? And ecstasy. Things would hurt when this light dimmed. The boy would change. But now in the sun she recognized him, and recognized that she did not know, and had never seen him, and loved him, in the bright new air with a simplicity she had never expected to know. "You," she said to him, skin for the first time on skin in the outside air, which was warm and shining, "you."

Women's Labors

LEE UPTON

You might want to be amused at the work
that is never done — or at our most difficult
labor, our work soonest ended.

In some work we are with most women,
crossing a bridge in our labor.
You will forgive me if I resort to Homer.

When the master returns,
the handmaidens are ordered
to clean up after the dead suitors,

washing blood from the tables,
the blood and water running from their sponges.
And then a cable is drawn about their waists,

and they are lifted from the ground
to perish in a great bunch together.
Even Homer must have pitied them:

a knot of slaves who only yesterday
laughed, believing the master
would always be missing.

How could I not pity them more —
slaves no one will defend.
If you are a woman in labor

waves break at the spine,
and a giant cable is drawn about your body.
You are held in the air for a very long time.

At last, later, you may be —
as I was — handed a daughter.
And for hours it seems there are no gods to claim us.

It is an illusion of course. But
even after the bracelet is clamped
upon the infant's wrist,

it seems we belong to no one.
We are out of history's singular lens.
for hours we serve no state, no master.

Notes from the Delivery Room

LINDA PASTAN

Strapped down,
victim in an old comic book,
I have been here before,
this place where pain winces
off the walls
like too bright light.
Bear down a doctor says,
foreman to sweating laborer,
but this work, this forcing
of one life from another
is something that I signed for
at a moment when I would have signed anything.
Babies should grow in fields;
common as beets or turnips
they should be picked and held
root end up, soil spilling
from between their toes —
and how much easier it would be later,
returning them to earth.
Bear up . . . bear down . . . the audience
grows restive, and I'm a new magician
who can't produce the rabbit
from my swollen hat.
She's crowning, someone says,
but there is no one royal here,
just me, quite barefoot,
greeting my barefoot child.

Giving Birth

MARGARET ATWOOD

But who gives it? And to whom is it given? Certainly it doesn't feel like giving, which implies a flow, a gentle handing over, no coercion. But there is scant gentleness here, it's too strenuous, the belly like a knotted fist, squeezing, the heavy trudge of the heart, every muscle in the body tight and moving, as in a slow motion shot of a high-jump, the faceless body sailing up, turning, hanging for a moment in the air, and then — back to real time again — the plunge, the rush down, the result. Maybe the phrase was made by someone viewing the result only: in this case, the rows of babies to whom birth has occurred, lying like neat packages in their expertly wrapped blankets, pink or blue, with their labels scotch-taped to their clear plastic cots, behind the plate-glass window.

No one ever says *giving death*, although they are in some ways the same, events, not things. And *delivering*, that act the doctor is generally believed to perform: who delivers what? Is it the mother who is delivered, like a prisoner being released? Surely not; nor is the child delivered to the mother like a letter through a slot. How can you be both the sender and the receiver at once? Was someone in bondage, is someone made free? Thus language, muttering in its archaic tongues of something, yet one more thing, that needs to be renamed.

It won't be by me, though. These are the only words I have, I'm stuck with them, stuck in them. (That image of the tar sands, old tableau in the Royal Ontario Museum, second floor north, how persistent it is. Will I break free, or will I be sucked down, fossilized, a sabre-toothed tiger or lumbering brontosaurus who ventured out too far? Words ripple at my feet, black, sluggish, lethal. Let me try once more, before the sun gets me, before I starve or drown, while I can. It's only a tableau after all, it's only a metaphor. See, I can speak, I am not trapped, and you on your part can understand. So we will go ahead as if there were no problem about language.)

This story about giving birth is not about me. In order to convince you of that I should tell you what I did this morning, before I sat down at this desk —

a door on top of two filing cabinets, radio to the left, calendar to the right, these devices by which I place myself in time. I got up at twenty-to-seven, and, halfway down the stairs, met my daughter, who was ascending, autonomously she thought, actually in the arms of her father. We greeted each other with hugs and smiles; we then played with the alarm clock and the hot water bottle, a ritual we go through only on the days her father has to leave the house early to drive into the city. This ritual exists to give me the illusion that I am sleeping in. When she finally decided it was time for me to get up, she began pulling my hair. I got dressed while she explored the bathroom scales and the mysterious white altar of the toilet. I took her downstairs and we had the usual struggle over her clothes. Already she is wearing miniature jeans, miniature T-shirts. After this she fed herself: orange, banana, muffin, porridge.

We then went out to the sunporch, where we recognized anew, and by their names, the dog, the cats and the birds, bluejays and goldfinches at this time of year, which is winter. She puts her fingers on my lips as I pronounce these words; she hasn't yet learned the secret of making them. I am waiting for her first word: surely it will be miraculous, something that has never yet been said. But if so, perhaps she's already said it and I, in my entrapment, my addiction to the usual, have not heard it.

In her playpen I discovered the first alarming thing of the day. It was a small naked woman, made of that soft plastic from which jiggly spiders and lizards and the other things people hang in their car windows are also made. She was given to my daughter by a friend, a woman who does props for movies, she was supposed to have been a prop but she wasn't used. The baby loved her and would crawl around the floor holding her in her mouth like a dog carrying a bone, with the head sticking out one side and the feet out the other. She seemed chewy and harmless, but the other day I noticed that the baby had managed to make a tear in the body with her new teeth. I put the woman into the cardboard box I use for toy storage.

But this morning she was back in the playpen and the feet were gone. The baby must have eaten them, and I worried about whether or not the plastic would dissolve in her stomach, whether it was toxic. Sooner or later, in the contents of her diaper, which I examine with the usual amount of maternal brooding, I knew I would find two small pink plastic feet. I removed the doll and later, while she was still singing to the dog outside the window, dropped it into the garbage. I am not up to finding tiny female arms, breasts, a head, in my daughter's disposable diapers, partially covered by undigested carrots and the husks of raisins, like the relics of some gruesome and demented murder.

Now she's having her nap and I am writing this story. From what I have said, you can see that my life (despite these occasional surprises, reminders of another world) is calm and orderly, suffused with that warm, reddish light, those well-placed blue highlights and reflecting surfaces (mirrors, plates, oblong window panes) you think of as belonging to Dutch genre paintings; and like them it is realistic in detail and slightly sentimental. Or at least it has an aura of sentiment. (Already I'm having moments of muted grief over those of my daughter's baby clothes which are too small for her to wear any more. I will be a keeper of hair, I will store things in trunks, I will weep over photos.) But above all it's solid, everything here has solidity. No more of those washes of light, those shifts, nebulous effects of cloud, Turner sunsets, vague fears, the impalpables Jeannie used to concern herself with.

I call this woman Jeannie after the song. I can't remember any more of the song, only the title. The point (for in language there are always these "points," these reflections; this is what makes it so rich and sticky, this is why so many have disappeared beneath its dark and shining surface, why you should never try to see your own reflection in it; you will lean over too far, a strand of your hair will fall in and come out gold, and, thinking it is gold all the way down, you yourself will follow, sliding into those outstretched arms, towards the mouth you think is opening to pronounce your name but instead, just before your ears fill with pure sound, will form a word you have never heard before . . .)

The point, for me, is in the hair. My own hair is not light brown, but Jeannie's was. This is one difference between us. The other point is the dreaming, for Jeannie isn't real in the same way that I am real. But by now, and I mean your time, both of us will have the same degree of reality, we will be equal: wraiths, echoes, reverberations in your own brain. At the moment though Jeannie is to me as I will some day be to you. So she is real enough.

Jeannie is on her way to the hospital, to give birth, to be delivered. She is not quibbling over these terms. She's sitting in the back seat of the car, with her eyes closed and her coat spread over her like a blanket. She is doing her breathing exercises and timing her contractions with a stopwatch. She has been up since two-thirty in the morning, when she took a bath and ate some lime Jell-O, and it's now almost ten. She has learned to count, during the slow breathing, in numbers (from one to ten while breathing in, from ten to one while breathing out) which she can actually see while she is silently pronouncing them. Each number is a different colour and, if she's concentrating very hard, a different typeface. They range from plain Roman to ornamented circus numbers, red with gold filigree and dots. This is a refinement not mentioned in any of the numerous books she's read on the subject. Jeannie is a devotee of handbooks. She has at least two shelves of books that cover everything from building kitchen cabinets to auto repairs to smoking your own hams. She doesn't do many of these things, but she does some of them, and in her suitcase, along with a washcloth, a package of lemon Lifesavers, a pair of glasses, a hot water bottle, some talcum powder and a paper bag, is the book that suggested she take along all of these things.

(By this time you may be thinking that I've invented Jeannie in order to distance myself from these experiences. Nothing could be further from the truth. I am, in fact, trying to bring myself closer to something that time has already made distant. As for Jeannie, my intention is simple: I am bringing her back to life.)

There are two other people in the car with Jeannie. One is a man, whom I will call A., for convenience. A. is driving. When Jeannie opens her eyes, at the end of every contraction, she can see the back of his slightly balding head and his reassuring shoulders. A. drives well and not too quickly. From time to time he asks her how she is, and she tells him how long the contractions are lasting and how long there is between them. When they stop for gas he buys them each a Styrofoam container of coffee. For months he has helped her with the breathing exercises, pressing on her knee as recommended by the book, and he will be present at the delivery. (Perhaps it's to him that the birth will be given, in the same sense that one gives a performance.) Together they have toured the hospital maternity ward, in company with a small group of other pairs like them: one thin solicitous person, one slow bulbous person. They have been shown the rooms, shared and private, the sitz-baths, the delivery room itself, which gave the impression of being white. The nurse was light-brown, with limber hips and elbows; she laughed a lot as she answered questions.

"First they'll give you an enema. You know what it is? They take a tube of water and put it up your behind. Now, the gentlemen must put on this — and these, over your shoes. And these hats, this one for those with long hair, this for those with short hair."

"What about those with no hair?" says A.

The nurse looks up at his head and laughs. "Oh, you still have some," she said. "If you have a question, do not be afraid to ask."

They have also seen the film made by the hospital, a full-colour film of a woman giving birth to, can it be a baby? "Not all babies will be this large at birth," the Australian nurse who introduces the movie says. Still, the audience, half of which is pregnant, doesn't look very relaxed when the lights go on. ("If you don't like the visuals," a friend of Jeannie's has told her, "you can always close your eyes.") It isn't the blood so much as the brownish-red disinfectant that bothers her. "I've decided to call this whole thing off," she says to A., smiling to show it's a joke. He gives her a hug and says, "Everything's going to be fine."

And she knows it is. Everything will be fine. But there is another woman in the car. She's sitting in the front seat, and she hasn't turned or acknowledged Jeannie in any way. She, like Jeannie, is going to the hospital. She too is pregnant. She is not going to the hospital to give birth, however, because the word, the words, are too alien to her experience, the experience she is about to have, to be used about it at all. She's wearing a cloth coat with checks in maroon and brown, and she has a kerchief tied over her hair. Jeannie has seen her before, but she knows little about her except that she is a woman who did not wish to become pregnant, who did not choose to divide herself like this, who did not choose any of these ordeals, these initiations. It would be no use telling her that everything is going to be fine. The word in English for unwanted intercourse is rape, but there is no word in the language for what is about to happen to this woman.

Jeannie has seen this woman from time to time throughout her pregnancy, always in the same coat, always with the same kerchief. Naturally, being pregnant herself has made her more aware of other pregnant women, and she has watched them, examined them covertly, every time she has seen one. But not every other pregnant woman is this woman. She did not, for instance, attend Jeannie's prenatal classes at the hospital, where the women were all young, younger than Jeannie.

"How many will be breastfeeding?" asks the Australian nurse with the hefty shoulders.

All hands but one shoot up. A modern group, the new generation, and the one lone bottle-feeder, who might have (who knows?) something wrong with her breasts, is ashamed of herself. The others look politely away from her. What they want most to discuss, it seems, are the differences between one kind of disposable diaper and another. Sometimes they lie on mats and squeeze each other's hands, simulating contractions and counting breaths. It's all very hopeful. The Australian nurse tells them not to get in and out of the bathtub by themselves. At the end of an hour they are each given a glass of apple juice.

There is only one woman in the class who has already given birth. She's there, she says, to make sure they give her a shot this time. They delayed it last time and she went through hell. The others look at her with mild disapproval. *They* are not clamouring for shots, they do not intend to go through hell. Hell comes from the wrong attitude, they feel. The books talk about *discomfort*.

"It's not discomfort, it's pain, baby," the woman says.

The others smile uneasily and the conversation slides back to disposable diapers.

Vitaminized, conscientious, well-read Jeannie, who has managed to avoid morning sickness, varicose veins, stretch marks, toxemia, and depression, who has had no aberrations of appetite, no blurrings of vision—why is she followed, then, by this other? At first it was only a glimpse now and then, at the infants' clothing section in Simpson's Basement, in the supermarket lineup, on streetcorners as she herself slid by in A.'s car: the haggard face, the bloated torso, the kerchief holding back the too-sparse hair. In any case, it was Jeannie who saw her, not the other way around. If she knew she was following Jeannie she gave no sign.

As Jeannie has come closer and closer to this day, the unknown day on which she will give birth, as time has thickened around her so that it has become something she must propel herself through, a kind of slush, wet earth underfoot, she has seen this woman more and more often, though always from a distance. Depending on the light, she has appeared by turns as a young girl of perhaps twenty to an older woman of forty or forty-five, but there was never any doubt in Jeannie's mind that it was the same woman. In fact it did not occur to her that the woman was not real in the usual sense (and perhaps she was, originally, on the first or second sighting, as the voice that causes an echo is real), until A. stopped for a red light during this drive to the hospital and the woman, who had been standing on the corner with a brown paper bag in her arms, simply opened the front door of the car and got in. A. didn't react, and Jeannie knows better than to say anything to him. She is aware that the woman is not really there: Jeannie is not crazy. She could even make the woman disappear by opening her eyes wider, by staring, but it is only the shape that would go away, not the feeling. Jeannie isn't exactly afraid of this woman. She is afraid for her.

When they reach the hospital, the woman gets out of the car and is through the door by the time A. has come around to help Jeannie out of the back seat. In the lobby she is nowhere to be seen. Jeannie goes through Admission in the usual way, unshadowed.

There has been an epidemic of babies during the night and the maternity ward is overcrowded. Jeannie waits for her room behind a dividing screen. Nearby someone is screaming, screaming and mumbling between screams in what sounds like a foreign language. Portuguese, Jeannie thinks. She tells herself that for them it is different, you're supposed to scream, you're regarded as queer if you don't scream, it's a required part of giving birth. Nevertheless she knows that the woman screaming is the other woman and she is screaming from pain. Jeannie listens to the other voice, also a woman's, comforting, reassuring: her mother? A nurse?

A. arrives and they sit uneasily, listening to the screams. Finally Jeannie is sent for and she goes for her prep. *Prep school*, she thinks. She takes off her clothes — when will she see them again? — and puts on the hospital gown. She is examined, labelled around the wrist, and given an enema. She tells the nurse she can't take Demerol because she's allergic to it, and the nurse writes this down. Jeannie doesn't know whether this is true or not but she doesn't want Demerol, she has read the books. She intends to put up a struggle over her pubic hair—surely she will lose her strength if it is all shaved off—but it turns out the nurse doesn't have very strong feelings about it. She is told her contractions are not far enough along to be taken seriously, she can even have lunch. She puts on her dressing gown and rejoins A., in the freshly vacated room, eats some tomato soup and a veal cutlet, and decides to take a nap while A. goes out for supplies.

Jeannie wakes up when A. comes back. He has brought a paper, some detective novels for Jeannie, and a bottle of Scotch for himself. A. reads the paper and drinks Scotch, and Jeannie reads *Poirot's Early Cases*. There is no connection between Poirot and her labour, which is now intensifying, unless it is the egg-shape of Poirot's head and the vegetable marrows he is known to cultivate with strands of wet wool (placentae? umbilical cords?). She is glad the stories are short; she is walking around the room now, between contractions. Lunch was definitely a mistake.

"I think I have back labour," she says to A. They get out the handbook and look up the instructions for this. It's useful that everything has a name. Jeannie kneels on the bed and rests her forehead on her arms while A. rubs her back. A. pours himself another Scotch, in the hospital glass. The nurse, in pink, comes, looks, asks about the timing, and goes away again. Jeannie is beginning to sweat. She can only manage half a page or so of Poirot before she has to clamber back up on the bed again and begin breathing and running through the coloured numbers.

When the nurse comes back, she has a wheelchair. It's time to go down to the labour room, she says. Jeannie feels stupid sitting in the wheelchair. She tells herself about peasant women having babies in the fields, Indian women having them on portages with hardly a second thought. She feels effete. But the hospital wants her to ride, and considering the fact that the nurse is tiny, perhaps it's just as well. What if Jeannie were to collapse, after all? After all her courageous talk. An image of the tiny pink nurse, ant-like, trundling large Jeannie through the corridors, rolling her along like a heavy beachball.

As they go by the check-in desk a woman is wheeled past on a table, covered by a sheet. Her eyes are closed and there's a bottle feeding into her arm through a tube. Something is wrong. Jeannie looks back—she thinks it was the other woman—but the sheeted table is hidden now behind the counter.

In the dim labour room Jeannie takes off her dressing gown and is helped up onto the bed by the nurse. A. brings her suitcase, which is not a suitcase actually but a small flight bag; the significance of this has not been lost on Jeannie, and in fact she now has some of the apprehensive feelings she associates with planes, including the fear of a crash. She takes out her Lifesavers, her glasses, her washcloth and the other things she thinks she will need. She removes her contact lenses and places them in their case, reminding A. that they must not be lost. Now she is purblind.

There is something else in her bag that she doesn't remove. It's a talisman, given to her several years ago as a souvenir by a travelling friend of hers. It's a rounded oblong of opaque blue glass, with four yellow and white eye shapes on it. In Turkey, her friend has told her, they hang them on mules to protect against the Evil Eye. Jeannie knows this talisman probably won't work for her, she is not Turkish and she isn't a mule, but it makes her feel safer to have it in the room with her. She had planned to hold it in her hand during the most difficult part of labour but somehow there is no longer any time for carrying out plans like this.

An old woman, a fat old woman dressed all in green, comes into the room and sits beside Jeannie. She says to A., who is sitting on the other side of Jeannie, "That is a good watch. They don't make watches like that any more." She is referring to his gold pocket watch, one of his few extravagances, which is on the night table. Then she places her hand on Jeannie's belly to feel the contraction. "This· is good," she says; her accent is Swedish or German. "This, I call a contraction. Before, it was nothing." Jeannie can no longer remember having seen her before. "Good. Good."

"When will I have it?" Jeannie asks, when she can talk, when she is no longer counting.

The old woman laughs. Surely that laugh, those tribal hands, have presided over a thousand beds, a thousand kitchen tables . . . "A long time yet," she says. "Eight, ten hours."

"But I've been *doing* this for twelve hours already," Jeannie says.

"Not hard labour," the woman says. "Not good, like this."

Jeannie settles into herself for the long wait. At the moment she can't remember why she wanted to have a baby in the first place. That decision was made by someone else, whose motives are now unclear. She remembers the way women who had babies used to smile at one another, mysteriously, as if there was something they knew that she didn't, the way they would casually exclude her from their frame of reference. What was the knowledge, the mystery, or was having a baby really no more inexplicable than having a car accident or an orgasm? (But these too were indescribable, events of the body, all of them; why should the mind distress itself trying to find a language for them?) She has sworn she will never do that to any woman without children, engage in those passwords and exclusions. She's old enough, she's been put through enough years of it to find it tiresome and cruel.

But — and this is the part of Jeannie that goes with the talisman hidden in her bag, not with the part that longs to build kitchen cabinets and smoke hams — she is, secretly, hoping for a mystery. Something more than this, something else, a vision. After all she is risking her life, though it's not too likely she will die. Still, some women do. Internal bleeding, shock, heart failure, a mistake on the part of someone, a nurse, a doctor. She deserves a vision, she deserves to be allowed to bring something back with her from this dark place into which she is now rapidly descending.

She thinks momentarily about the other woman. Her motives, too, are unclear. Why doesn't she want to have a baby? Has she been raped, does she have ten other children, is she starving? Why hasn't she had an abortion? Jeannie doesn't know, and in fact it no longer matters why. *Uncross your fingers,* Jeannie thinks to her. Her face, distorted with pain and terror, floats briefly behind Jeannie's eyes before it too drifts away.

Jeannie tries to reach down to the baby, as she has many times before, sending waves of love, colour, music, down through her arteries to it, but she finds she can no longer do this. She can no longer feel the baby as a baby, its arms and legs poking, kicking, turning. It has collected itself together, it's a hard sphere, it does not have time right now to listen to her. She's grateful for this because she isn't sure anyway how good the message would be. She no longer has control of the numbers either, she can no longer see them, although she continues mechanically to count. She realizes she has practised for the wrong thing, A. squeezing her knee was nothing, she should have practised for this, whatever it is.

"Slow down," A. says. She's on her side now, he's holding her hand. "Slow it right down."

"I can't, I can't do it, I can't do this."

"Yes you can."

"Will I sound like that?"

"Like what?" A. says. Perhaps he can't hear it: it's the other woman, in the room next door or the room next door to that. She's screaming and crying, screaming and crying. While she cries she is saying, over and over, "It hurts. It hurts."

"No, you won't," he says. So there is someone, after all.

A doctor comes in, not her own doctor. They want her to turn over on her back.

"I can't," she says. "I don't like it that way." Sounds have receded, she has trouble hearing them. She turns over and the doctor gropes with her rubber-gloved hand. Something wet and hot flows over her thighs.

"It was just ready to break," the doctor says. "All I had to do was touch it. Four centimetres," she says to A.

"Only *four*?" Jeannie says. She feels cheated; they must be wrong. The doctor says her own doctor will be called in time. Jeannie is outraged at them. They have not understood, but it's too late to say this and she slips back into the dark place, which is not hell, which is more like being inside, trying to get out. *Out*, she says or thinks. Then she is floating, the numbers are gone, if anyone told her to get up, go out of the room, stand on her head, she would do it. From minute to minute she comes up again, grabs for air.

"You're hyperventilating," A. says. "Slow it down." He is rubbing her back now, hard, and she takes his hand and shoves it viciously farther down, to the right place, which is not the right place as soon as his hand is there. She remembers a story she read once, about the Nazis tying the legs of Jewish women together during labour. She never really understood before how that could kill you.

A nurse appears with a needle. "I don't want it," Jeannie says.

"Don't be hard on yourself," the nurse says. "You don't have to go through pain like that." *What pain?* Jeannie thinks. When there is no pain she feels nothing, when there is pain, she feels nothing because there is no *she*. This, finally, is the disappearance of language. *You don't remember afterwards*, she has been told by almost everyone.

Jeannie comes out of a contraction, gropes for control. "Will it hurt the baby?" she says.

"It's a mild analgesic," the doctor says. "We wouldn't allow anything that would hurt the baby." Jeannie doesn't believe this. Nevertheless she is jabbed, and the doctor is right, it is very mild, because it doesn't seem to do a thing for Jeannie, though A. later tells her she has slept briefly between contractions.

Suddenly she sits bolt upright. She is wide awake and lucid. "You have to ring that bell right now," she says. "This baby is being born."

A. clearly doesn't believe her. "I can feel it, I can feel the head," she says. A. pushes the button for the call bell. A nurse appears and checks, and now everything is happening too soon, nobody is ready. They set off down the hall, the nurse wheeling. Jeannie feels fine. She watches the corridors, the edges of everything shadowy because she doesn't have her glasses on. She hopes A. will remember to bring them. They pass another doctor.

"Need me?" she asks.

"Oh no," the nurse answers breezily. "Natural childbirth."

Jeannie realizes that this woman must have been the anaesthetist. "What?" she says, but it's too late now, they are in the room itself, all those glossy surfaces, tubular strange apparatus like a science fiction movie, and the nurse is telling her to get onto the delivery table. No one else is in the room.

"You must be crazy," Jeannie says.

"Don't push," the nurse says.

"What do you mean?" Jeannie says. This is absurd. Why should she wait, why should the baby wait for them because they're late?

"Breathe through your mouth," the nurse says. "Pant," and Jeannie finally remembers how. When the contraction is over she uses the nurse's arm as a lever and hauls herself across onto the table.

From somewhere her own doctor materializes, in her doctor suit already, looking even more like Mary Poppins than usual, and Jeannie says, "Bet you weren't expecting to see me so soon!" The baby is being born when Jeannie said it would, though just three days ago the doctor said it would be at least another week, and this makes Jeannie feel jubilant and smug. Not that she knew, she'd believed the doctor.

She's being covered with a green tablecloth, they are taking far too long, she feels like pushing the baby out now, before they are ready. A. is there by her head, swathed in robes, hats, masks. He has forgotten her glasses. "Push now," the doctor says. Jeannie grips with her hands, grits her teeth, face, her whole body together, a snarl, a fierce smile, the baby is enormous, a stone, a boulder, her bones unlock, and, once, twice, the third time, she opens like a birdcage turning slowly inside out.

A pause; a wet kitten slithers between her legs. "Why don't you look?" says the doctor, but Jeannie still has her eyes closed. No glasses, she couldn't have seen a thing anyway. "Why don't you look?" the doctor says again.

Jeannie opens her eyes. She can see the baby, who has been wheeled up beside her and is fading already from the alarming birth purple. A *good baby*, she thinks, meaning it as the old woman did: *a good watch*, well-made, substantial. The baby isn't crying; she squints in the new light. Birth isn't something that has been given to her, nor has she taken it. It was just something that has happened so they could greet each other like this. The nurse is stringing beads for her name. When the baby is bundled and tucked beside Jeannie, she goes to sleep.

As for the vision, there wasn't one. Jeannie is conscious of no special knowledge; already she's forgetting what it was like. She's tired and very cold; she is shaking, and asks for another blanket. A. comes back to the room with her; her clothes are still there. Everything is quiet, the other woman is no longer screaming. Something has happened to her, Jeannie knows. Is she dead? Is the baby dead? Perhaps she is one of those casualties (and how can Jeannie herself be sure, yet, that she will not be among them) who will go into postpartum depression and never come out. "You see, there was nothing to be afraid of," A. says before he leaves, but he was wrong.

The next morning Jeannie wakes up when it's light. She's been warned about getting out of bed the first time without the help of a nurse, but she decides to do it anyway (peasant in the field! Indian on the portage!). She's still running on adrenalin; she's also weaker than she thought, but she wants very much to look out the window. She feels she's been inside too long, she wants to see the sun come up. Being awake this early always makes her feel a little unreal, a little insubstantial, as if she's partly transparent, partly dead.

(It was to me, after all, that the birth was given, Jeannie gave it, I am the result. What would she make of me? Would she be pleased?)

The window is two panes with a venetian blind sandwiched between them; it turns by a knob at the side. Jeannie has never seen a window like this before. She closes and opens the blind several times. Then she leaves it open and looks out.

All she can see from the window is a building. It's an old stone building, heavy and Victorian, with a copper roof oxidized to green. It's solid, hard, darkened by soot, dour, leaden. But as she looks at this building, so old and seemingly immutable, she sees that it's made of water. Water, and some tenuous jellylike substance. Light flows through it from behind (the sun is coming up), the building is so thin, so fragile, that it quivers in the slight dawn wind. Jeannie sees that if the building is this way (a touch could destroy it, a ripple of the earth, why has no one noticed, guarded it against accidents?) then the rest of the world must be like this too, the entire earth, the rocks, people, trees, everything needs to be protected, cared for, tended. The enormity of this task defeats her; she will never be up to it, and what will happen then?

Jeannie hears footsteps in the hall outside her door. She thinks it must be the other woman, in her brown and maroon checked coat, carrying her paper bag, leaving the hospital now that her job is done. She has seen Jeannie safely through, she must go now to hunt through the streets of the city for her next case. But the door opens, it's only a nurse, who is just in time to catch Jeannie as she sinks to the floor, holding onto the edge of the air-conditioning unit. The nurse scolds her for getting up too soon.

After that the baby is carried in, solid, substantial, packed together like an apple. Jeannie examines her, she is complete, and in the days that follow Jeannie herself becomes drifted over with new words, her hair slowly darkens, she ceases to be what she was and is replaced, gradually, by someone else.

After Giving Birth, I Recall the Madonna and Child

JULIANNA BAGGOTT

Who could ever believe it:
  the cows, shoulder to shoulder,
    lowing three-part harmony,
the stable so Hollywood-set tidy,
Joseph and Mary, serene, smiling,
and the boy, pink and fat, already blessing us
      with two tiny fingers raised
from his white swaddle?

He's never purple, blood-stained,
      yellowed — like my babies —
      from swimming in his own shit.

Maybe if we could see her belly
hardened by contraction,
      her knees
          spread, steam rising
from the wash of blood,
and her face contorted with pain,
the cords of her neck
          taut and blue,
then we might believe Joseph,
how he must have said,
      I can see the head.
          It's glowing.

Delivering Lily

PHILLIP LOPATE

Ever since expectant fathers were admitted into delivery rooms a few decades ago, they have come armed with video cameras and awe. Before I became a father, I often heard men describe seeing the birth of their baby as "transcendental," the greatest experience in their lives. They would recall how choked up they got, even boast about their tears . . . it sounded very kitschy, like the ultimate sunrise. Being a non-transcendentalist, with suspicions, moreover, about my affective capacities, I was unsure how I would react. I had seen birthing scenes often enough in movies: How much more surprising could the reality be? I wondered, as someone who used to pass out at the sight of my own blood filling syringes, would I prove useless and faint? Or would I rise to the occasion, and be so moved in the bargain that at last I could retire those definitions of myself as a detached skeptic and accept the sweet, decent guy allegedly underneath?

Whatever reactions would befall me, I prepared myself for a minor role. The star of any birth is the mother, her co-star, Baby, her supporting leads, the medics. At nativity, every father feels himself a Joseph.

Sept. 16, 1994, around 4 in the afternoon, I came across my wife, Cheryl, lying on the couch. She said she had "spotted" earlier, and wondered if this teaspoon's worth of sanguineous discharge could be what the books referred to, more scarletly, as "the bloody show."

I had already made a date with a friend—poet and fellow Brooklynite Harvey Shapiro—to attend the end of Yom Kippur services at the local temple, after which I was to bring Harvey back to our house to break fast together. Harvey would supply the traditional challah bread and herring, and Cheryl the rest of the meal. I promised her I would return with Harvey no later than 7.

At the Kane Street Synagogue, the rabbi was taking her own sweet time, and I knew Cheryl would be annoyed if her dinner got cold, so I prevailed on Harvey to leave the service early. Just as well. We were sitting around the table, getting ready to enjoy Cheryl's lamb and baked potatoes, when she pointed mysteriously to her belly.

"What's up?" I asked.

"I think it's starting."

She smiled. If it was indeed starting, she could skip her appointment the following week for an artificial induction. The fetus was at a good weight, and the doctors hadn't wanted to take the chance of the placenta breaking down, as happened often with overdue deliveries. Cheryl had felt sad at the thought of being artificially induced — missing the suspense of those first contractions — but now the baby seemed to be arriving on her due date, which meant we were in for the whole "natural" experience after all.

First-time parents, we had wondered whether we would really be able to tell when it was time. Would we embarrass ourselves by rushing off to the hospital days early, at the first false quiver? How to be sure whether the sensations Cheryl reported were the contractions? As instructed, we began timing them. Meanwhile, our downstairs neighbor Beth popped in, and stayed to witness potential history.

Harvey, a man in his late 60s and a grizzled veteran of parenthood, distracted us with stories of his boys' infancies while I kept my eye on the second hand. The contractions seemed to be spaced between five and seven minutes apart. We phoned our obstetricians. The office was closed for the Jewish holiday, but the answering service relayed the message to Dr. Arita, who was on call that night. Dr. Arita told Cheryl not to come into the hospital until contractions began occurring regularly, at five minutes apart, and lasted a full minute.

As soon as we had clocked two one-minute contractions in a row, I was impatient to start for the hospital. I had no wish to deliver a baby on the kitchen floor. Cheryl seemed calmer as she described her condition to Dr. Arita. It was now 10 P.M., and he told her she would probably be coming into the hospital "sometime that night." This phraseology sounded too vague to me. I marveled at my wife's self-possessed demeanor. Cheryl was manifesting her sweet, lovely, modest, cheerfully plucky side — the side she presented to my friends and to outsiders; it was not a lie, but it gave no hint of her other self, that anxious, morose perfectionist she often produced when we were alone.

At 10:30 the contractions began to arrive five minutes apart, and with more sharpness. Arita, beeped, said to come in. I pulled together a few last items (rubber ball, ice pack) on the checklist of what to take to the delivery room, and, saying goodbye to our guests, had gotten halfway to the door when I noticed Cheryl was, as usual, not quite ready to leave the house. She decided she had to water the mums.

For months, we had debated which neighborhood car service to call for the hour-long trip from Carroll Gardens to Mount Sinai Hospital, on the Upper East Side of Manhattan. Cheryl, a superb driver with no faith in my own lesser automotive skills, had even considered taking the wheel herself when the time came. Now suddenly she turned to me and said, "You drive. Just don't speed."

I maneuvered the car with caution over the Brooklyn Bridge, then up the FDR Drive, while Cheryl spoke happily of feeling empowered and in control. The contractions, she said, were not that painful: "I like these intense experiences that put you in contact with life and death." Premature bravado, I thought, but kept this to myself, glad to have her confidently chatting away; it meant she wouldn't have as much chance to find fault with my driving.

We parked the car in the hospital's indoor lot. Cheryl began walking very slowly up the ramp, holding her back. "I can't walk any faster," she snapped (the first sign of a change in mood?), as if responding to an unspoken criticism she sensed me making about her pace, when in fact, I was stumbling all over myself to support her.

It was close to midnight as we entered the eerily quiet Klingenstein Pavilion. I approached the security guard, busy flirting with a nurse's aide, for directions. We had pre-registered weeks before to avoid red tape at zero hour. After signing in, we were directed down a long creepy corridor into Birthing Room C. Mount Sinai Hospital has one of the largest maternity wards in the country, which is one reason we chose it; but suddenly its very magnitude made us uneasy. We felt no longer dramatic or special, but merely one more on the assembly line, popping babies up and down the hall.

The expectant couple was deposited in Room C, and left alone. It would be difficult to describe Room C except in regard to absences: It was not cozy, it was not charming, it was not tiny, it was not big, it was not even decrepit, it had nothing for the eye to fasten on. It was what you expected, more or less, of an anonymous hospital room with a quick turnover; but Cheryl, I sensed, had hoped for more — more ambiance, amenities, *something* for the money. A visual designer by trade, she could, I knew, be preternaturally sensitive to new environments. Like a bride who finds herself in a nondescript wedding chapel, Cheryl may have long nurtured a fantasy of the ideal first-time birthing chamber, and something told me this was not it.

Often I allow myself to be made captive of my wife's moods, registering in an instant her first signs of discontent, and trying (usually without success) to gentle her out of it. I suspect that this catering to her anxiety — if only by playing the optimist to her pessimist — is really laziness on my part: It saves me the trouble of having to initiate emotions on my own.

Cheryl was given a hospital gown to wear. The moment she put it on, her confidence evaporated. She became an object, a thing to cut open. I cast about for ways to regain the light mood we had had in the car, but it was no use. "Let's get out of this room. It gives me the willies," she said.

We went for a walk around the ward, opening doors and peering inside like naughty children. Our best discovery was a conference room, dark and coffee-machined and air-conditioned — freezing, in fact — which suited her just fine. We hid out for 15 minutes in this non-medical haven. But her contractions eventually drove us back to Room C.

Cheryl lay down. She took an instant dislike to her berth, saying, "I don't like this bed!" and fiddling with the dials to raise and lower it. (An aversion, I thought, to proneness itself, which brought with it the surrender of her last sense of control.) I turned on the TV to distract her. The second half of "Working Girl," with Melanie Griffith, was on; Cheryl said she didn't want to hear the dialogue, so I was just to keep the sound loud enough to provide a background of "white noise." This was certainly a temperamental difference between us: If I had been giving birth, whatever the ordeal, I think I would have wanted the dialogue as well as the visuals of the movie on television. But I obliged; besides, we had already seen it.

For some reason, I had imagined our being swamped by medical personnel the moment we entered the hospital. We had not anticipated these quarter-hours of waiting alone, without instructions. We sat about like useless tourists who arrive in an economy hotel after a long trip, too tired to attempt the streets of a foreign city, yet too hemmed-in by the unlovely room to enjoy a siesta.

How glad we were to see Dr. Arita walk in! A silver-mustached, suavely Latin, aristocratic type, he was one of Cheryl's favorites on the team. (She had been instructed to "establish a rapport" with all four obstetricians, since you never knew who was going to be on call during the actual delivery.) Cheryl had once admitted to me she thought Arita handsome, which made me a little jealous of him. He wore the standard green cotton scrubs with "Property of Mt. Sinai Hospital" printed on the material (still wrinkled, pulled straight from the dryer, no doubt: In former times, they would have been crisply ironed, to maintain authority and morale) and, improbably, had on a shower cap, which suggested he had come straight from surgery; this fashion accessory, I was happy to see, reduced somewhat his matinee-idol appeal.

It was Dr. Arita who had, months before, performed the amniocentesis, which ascertained among other things that our baby was to be a girl. Dr. Arita had a clinical terseness, never taking five words to say what four could accomplish. He asked Cheryl if she wanted Demerol to cut the pain and help her sleep.

Cheryl had her speech all ready. "No, I don't want Demerol. Demerol will make me groggy. It'll turn my brain to mush, and I hate that sensation."

"All right. If you change your mind, let me know." With those succinct words, he exited.

From time to time a nurse would see how Cheryl was getting along. Or the resident on the floor would pop in and say, "You're doing great, you're doing great!" Increasingly, Cheryl wasn't. Her contractions had become much more intense, and she began making a gesture with her hands of climbing the wall of pain, reaching her arms toward the ceiling. Finally she cried out:

"Painkiller. Painkiller. DEMEROL."

I ran to fetch the resident.

"I'd give it to my wife," he said, which seemed to soothe Cheryl somewhat. Exhausted by her pain, she had entered a cone of self-absorption, and only a doctor's or nurse's words seemed able to reach her. She had tuned me out, I thought, except as a potential irritant—a lowly servant who was not doing his job. "More ice," she said, rattling the cup as though scornful of the lousy service in this joint.

During prenatal Lamaze pep talks, the husband was always being built up as an essential partner in the birthing process. This propaganda about the husband's importance, the misapplied fallout of equal sharing of domestic responsibilities in modern marriage, struck me as bunk, since the husband's parturient chores appeared menial at best. One of my spousal duties was to replenish the ice that Cheryl sucked on or rubbed across her forehead. Throughout the night I made a dozen of these ice runs, dashing into the kitchenette and filling the cup with chips. Back in the room, Cheryl would cry out "Ice," then "ice, ice!" with mounting urgency, as though the seconds between her request and my compliance were an eternity marking my bottomless clumsiness. I was rushing as fast as I could (though I must confess that when someone yells at me to fetch something or perform any manual action, it releases a slight physical hesitation on my part, perhaps no longer than 1.5 seconds, but this 1.5-second delay was enough to drive Cheryl wild. It is, you might say, the 1.5 second factor that makes conjugal life so continuously absorbing). Also, if I gave her a piece she deemed too small or too large, she would berate me in tones of "How could you be so stupid?" This went on for hours.

Her underlying reproach seemed to be that I was not hooked into her brain — was not able to anticipate her needs through ESP or heightened sensitivity — and she would have to waste precious breath articulating them. I would occasionally try to ease the tension by giving her a neck rub or caressing her hand, all recommended consolations by the Lamaze instructor. She shook me off like a cockroach. We husbands had been instructed as well to make "eye contact" with our wives: But whenever I tried this, Cheryl acquired the look of a runaway horse made acutely distressed by an unwanted obstacle in her path.

Sadly, I was not sufficiently generous to rise above feelings of being unfairly attacked. Days later, it surprised me to hear Cheryl telling people I had been wonderful during labor: "like a rock." Why, if this was so, I asked her, had she been so mean to me at the time? She explained rather reasonably that she was just taking her pain and putting it on me as fast as possible.

Sometimes, during contractions, she would literally transfer her pain to me by gouging my leg. Mistakenly thinking she was attached to my foot, I offered it to her, only to have it pushed away. "No, not the foot, I don't want the foot, I want the hand!" she screamed. (Being abnormally sensitive to smells all during pregnancy, she had picked up an unpleasant odor from my socks.)

What she liked best, it turned out, was to grip my trousers belt and yank hard. Eventually we worked out a routine: As soon as she started climbing a contraction, I would jump out of my chair, which was on her left side, run over to her right side and stand beside her as she pulled and thrashed at my belt for the duration of the spasm. All the while I would be counting off every five seconds of the contraction. I was not entirely sure what purpose I served by counting aloud in this fashion; they had told us husbands to do so in Lamaze class, in connection with certain breathing exercises, but since we had thrown those exercises out the window soon after coming to the hospital, why, I wondered, was it necessary to keep up a count?

I should explain that we had never been ideal Lamaze students. Too preoccupied with our lives to practice the breathing regularly at home, or perhaps unable to overcome the feeling that it was a bit silly, when the actual labor came, it was so unremitting that we could not be bothered trying to execute these elegant respiratory tempi. It would be like asking a drowning woman to waltz. Cheryl continued to breathe, willy nilly; that seemed enough for both of us. (I can hear the Lamaze people saying: Yes, but if only you had followed our instructions, it would have been so much easier . . .) In any event, I would call out bogus numbers to please Cheryl, sensing that the real point of this exercise was for her to have the reassurance of my voice, measuring points on the arc of her pain, as proof that I was equally focused with her on the same experience.

In spite of, or because of, this excruciating workout, we were both getting very sleepy. The wee hours of the morning, from 2 to 6 A.M., saw the surreal mixture of agony merging with drowsiness. Cheryl would be contorted with pain, and I could barely stop from yawning in her face. She too would doze off, between contractions: Waking suddenly as though finding herself on a steeply ascending roller coaster, she would yowl Ooowwwww! I'd snap awake, stare at my watch, call out a number, rush to the other side of the bed and present my belt for yanking. When it was over I would go back to my chair and nod off again, to the sound of some ancient TV rerun. I recall Erik Estrada hopping on a motorcycle in "C.H.I.P.S.," and "Hawaii Five-O's" lead-in music; and early morning catnap dreams punctuated by a long spate of CNN, discussing the imminent invasion of Haiti; then CBS News, Dan Rather's interview with the imperturbable dictator, Raoul Cedras, and "Ice, *ice!*"

During this long night, Cheryl put her head against my shoulder and I stroked her hair for a long while. This tenderness was as much a part of the experience as the irritation, though I seem to recall it less. It went without saying that we loved each other, were tied together; and perhaps the true meaning of intimacy was not to have to put on a mask of courtesy in situations like these.

Demerol had failed to kill the pain: Cheryl began screaming "PAIN-KILLER, PAINKILLER, HELP," in that telegraphic style dictated by her contractions. I tracked down the resident, and got him to give her a second dose of Demerol. But less than an hour after, her pain had reached a knuckle-biting pitch beyond Demerol's ministrations. At 6 in the morning, I begged the doctors to administer an epidural, which would numb Cheryl from the waist down. "Epidural" — the open sesame we had committed to memory in the unlikely event of unbearable pain — was guaranteed to be effective, but the doctors tried to defer this as long as possible, because the numbness in her legs would make it harder to push the baby out during the active phase. (My mind was too fatigued to grasp ironies, but it perked up at this word "active," which implied that all the harsh turmoil Cheryl and I had undergone for what seemed like forever, was merely the latent, "passive" phase of labor.)

The problem, the reason the labor was taking so long, was that while Cheryl had entered the hospital with a membrane 80 percent "effaced," her cervix was still very tight, dilated only one centimeter. From midnight to about 5 in the morning, the area had expanded from one to only two centimeters; she needed to get to 10 centimeters before delivery could occur. To speed the process, she was now given an inducement drug, Proactin — a very small amount, since this medication is powerful enough to cause seizures. The anesthesiologist also hooked Cheryl up to an IV for her epidural, which was to be administered by drops, not all at once, so that it would last longer.

Blessedly, it did its job.

Around 7 in the morning Cheryl was much calmer, thanks to the epidural. She sent me out to get some breakfast. I never would have forgiven myself if I had missed the baby's birth while dallying over coffee, but Cheryl's small dilation encouraged me to take the chance. Around the corner from the hospital was a Greek coffee shop, Peter's, where I repaired and ate a cheese omelette and read the morning *Times*. I can't remember if I did the crossword puzzle: Knowing me, I probably did, relishing these quiet 40 minutes away from the hospital, and counting on them to refresh me for whatever exertions lay ahead.

Back on the floor, I ran into Dr. Raymond Sandler, Cheryl's favorite obstetrician on the team. Youthfully gray-haired, with a melodious South African accent and kind brown eyes, he said the same things the other doctors did, but they came out sounding warmer. Now, munching on some food, he said, "She looks good!" Dr. Sandler thought the baby would come out by noon. If so, delivery would occur during his shift. I rushed off to tell Cheryl the good news.

Momentarily not in pain, she smiled weakly as I held her hand. Our attention drifted to the morning talk shows. (Cheryl had long ago permitted me to turn up the volume.) Redheaded Marilu Henner was asking three gorgeous soap opera actresses how they kept the zip in their marriage. What were their secret ways of turning on their husbands? One had the honesty to admit that, ever since the arrival of their baby, sex had taken a backseat to exhaustion and nursing. I liked her for saying that, wondering at the same time what sacrifices were in store for Cheryl and me. Marilu (I had never watched her show before, but now I felt like a regular) moved on to the question, what first attracted each woman to her husband. "His tight buns." The audience loved it. I glanced over at Cheryl, to see how she was taking this: She was leaning to one side with a concentrated expression of oncoming nausea, her normally beautiful face looking drawn, hatchet-thin. She seemed to defy the laws of perspective: a Giacometti face floating above a Botero stomach.

We were less like lovers at that moment than like two soldiers who had marched all night and fallen out, panting, by the side of the road. The titillations of the TV show could have come from another planet, so far removed did it feel from us; that eros had gotten us here in the first place seemed a rumor at best.

Stubbornly, in this antiseptic, torture-witnessing cubicle, I tried to recover the memory of sexual feeling. I thought about how often we'd made love in order to conceive this baby — every other night, just to be on the safe side, during the key weeks of the month. At first we were frisky, reveling in it like newlyweds. Later, it became another chore to perform, like moving the car for alternate-side-of-the-street parking, but with the added fear that all our efforts might be in vain. Cheryl was 38, I was 50. We knew many other couples around our age who were trying, often futilely, to conceive — a whole generation, it sometimes seemed, of careerists who had put off childbearing for years, and now wanted more than anything a child of their own, and were deep into sperm motility tests, *in vitro* fertilizations and the lot. After seven months of using the traditional method, and suffering one miscarriage in the process, we were just about to turn ourselves over like lab rats to the fertility experts when Cheryl got pregnant. This time it took. Whatever torment labor brought, we could never forget for a moment how privileged we were to be here.

"You've got to decide about her middle name!" Cheryl said with groggy insistence, breaking the silence.

"OK. Just relax, we will."

"Elena? Francesca? Come on, Phillip, we've got to get this taken care of or we'll be screwed."

"We won't be 'screwed.' If worse comes to worse, I'll put both names down."

"But we have to make up our minds. We can't just —"

"Well, which name do you prefer?"

"I can't think straight now."

A new nurse came on the day shift: a strong, skillful West Indian woman named Jackie, who looked only about 40 but who told us later that she was a grandmother. As it turned out, she would stay with us to the end, and we would become abjectly dependent on her — this stranger who had meant nothing to us a day before, and whom we would never see again.

At nine centimeters' dilation, and with Jackie's help, Cheryl started to push. "Pretend you are going to the toilet," Jackie told Cheryl, who obeyed, evacuating a foul-smelling liquid.

"She made a bowel movement, that's good," Dr. Sandler commented in his reassuring way. Jackie wiped it up with a towelette, and we waited for the next contraction. Jackie would say with her island accent, "Push, push in the bottom," calling to my mind that disco song, "Push, Push in the Bush." Cheryl would make a supreme effort. But now a new worry arose: The fetal monitor was reporting a slower heartbeat after each contraction, which suggested a decrease in the baby's oxygen. You could hear the baby's heartbeat amplified in the room, like rain on a tin roof, and every time the sound slowed down, you panicked.

Dr. Sandler ordered a blood sample taken from the infant's scalp, to see if she was properly aerated (i.e., getting enough oxygen). In addition, a second fetal monitor was attached to the fetus's scalp (don't ask me how). My poor baby, for whom it was not enough to undergo the birth trauma, was having to endure the added insult of getting bled while still in the womb.

The results of the blood test were positive: "Not to worry," Dr. Sandler said. But just in case, he ordered Cheryl to wear an oxygen mask for the remainder of the labor. This oxygen mask frightened us, with its bomb shelter associations.

"How will the baby be delivered?" Cheryl asked, as the apparatus was placed over her face. "Will they have to use forceps?"

"That will depend on your pushing," answered Dr. Sandler, and then he left. I did not like the self-righteous sound of this answer, implying it was ours to screw up or get right. We had entrusted ourselves to the medical profession precisely so that they could take care of everything for us!

Often, after a push, the towelette underneath Cheryl was spattered with blood. Jackie would swoop it up, throw it on the floor, kick it out of the way, raise Cheryl's lower half from the bed and place a fresh towelette underneath. The floor began to smell like a battleground, with blood and shit underfoot.

"Push harder, push harder, harder, harder, harder," Jackie chanted in her Barbados accent. Then: "Keep going, keep going, keep going!" Cheryl's legs were floppy from the epidural; she reported a feeling of detachment from her body. In order for her to have a counter-pressure to push against, I was instructed to lift her left leg and double it against the crook of my arm. This maneuver, more difficult than it sounds, had to be sustained for several hours;

a few times I felt that my arm was going to snap and I might end up hospitalized as well. It was probably the hardest physical work I've ever done — though nothing compared, of course, to what Cheryl was going through. I feared she would burst a blood vessel.

Around 11, Jackie went on her lunch break, replaced by a nurse who seemed much less willing to get involved. A tense conversation ensued between Dr. Sandler and the new nurse:

"This patient is fully effaced," he said.

"My other patient is fully, too."

He sighed, she shrugged, and the next minute, they were both out the door. Left alone with a wife buckling in pain, I felt terrified and enraged: How dare Jackie take a food break now? Couldn't we page her in the cafeteria and tell her to get her ass back? It was no use, I had to guide Cheryl through her contractions as if I knew what I was doing. This meant watching the fetal monitor printout for the start of each contraction (signaled by an elevating line), then lodging her leg against my arm, and chanting her through the three requisite pushes per contraction, without any firm idea exactly when each was supposed to occur. The first time I did this I got so engrossed pressing her leg hard against me that I forgot the cheerleading. I have a tendency to fall silent during crises, conserving energy for stock-taking and observation. This time I was brought up short by Cheryl yelling at me: "How am I supposed to know how long to push?" I wanted to answer: I'm not a trained medic, I have no idea myself. The next time, however, I bluffed, "Push, push in the bottom!" doing my best Jackie imitation until Jackie herself came back.

Sometime near noon, Dr. Sandler made an appearance with his colleague, Dr. Schiller, and began explaining the case to her. Cheryl had never felt as confident about Laura Schiller as she had about Dr. Sandler and Dr. Arita, either because Dr. Schiller was the only woman on the team (not that Cheryl would have agreed with this explanation), or because Dr. Schiller had a skinny, birdlike, tightly wound manner that did not immediately inspire tranquillity, or because the two women had simply not had the opportunity to "develop a rapport." With a sinking sensation, we began to perceive that Dr. Sandler was abandoning us. Actually, he probably would have been happy to deliver Lily, if only she had arrived when he had predicted, before noon.

Now he had to be somewhere else, so he turned the job over to his capable colleague.

Dr. Schiller brought in a younger woman — a resident or intern — and they discussed whether the baby was presenting OA or OR (whatever that meant). Now they turned to the expectant mother and got serious. Dr. Schiller proved to be a much tougher coach than Jackie. "Come on, Cheryl, you can try harder than *that*," she would say. Cheryl's face clouded over with intense effort, her veins stood out, and half the time her push was judged effective, the other half, not. I could never fathom the criteria used to separate the successes from the failures; all I knew was that my wife is no shirker, and I resented anyone implying she was. If some of Cheryl's pushes lacked vigor, it was because the epidural had robbed her of sensation below, and because the long night of pain, wasted on a scarcely increased dilation, had sapped her strength.

Over the next hour, doctor's and patient's rhythms synchronized, until something like complete trust developed between them. Dr. Schiller cajoled; Cheryl responded. We were down to basics; the procedure of birth had never seemed so primitive. I couldn't believe that here we were in the post-industrial era, and the mother still had to push the fetus by monstrously demanding effort, fractions of an inch down the vaginal canal. It was amazing that the human race survived, given such a ponderous childbearing method. With all of science's advances, delivering a baby still came down to three time-worn approaches: push, forceps or Caesarean.

This particular baby, it seemed, did not want to cross the perineum. "If the baby's no closer after three more pushes," Dr. Schiller declared, "We're going to have to go to forceps."

Forceps would necessitate an episiotomy — a straight surgical cut of the pubic region to keep it from fraying and tearing further. An episiotomy also would have Cheryl sore and unable to sit for weeks. Knowing that I would probably be accused of male insensitivity, and sensing my vote counted marginally at best, I nevertheless expressed a word in favor of forceps. Anything to shorten the ordeal and get the damn baby out. Cheryl had suffered painful contractions for 18 hours, she was exhausted, I was spent — and I was dying with curiosity to see my little one! I couldn't take the suspense any longer — obviously not a legitimate reason. Cheryl worried that the forceps might dent or misshape the baby's skull. Dr. Schiller explained that the chances of that occurring were very slight, given the improved design of modern instruments.

Cheryl pushed as hard as she could, three times, with a most desperate look in her eyes. No use.

"I always try to give a woman two hours at best to push the baby out. But if it doesn't work—then I go to forceps," Dr. Schiller said authoritatively. Cheryl looked defeated. "Okay, we'll try one more time. But now you really have to push. Give me the push of the day."

The Push of the Day must have felt like a tsunami to Lily, but she clung to the side of her underwater cave.

They readied the scalpel for an episiotomy. I turned away: Some things you can't bear to watch done to a loved one. Dr. Schiller, kneeling, looked inside Cheryl and cried out, "She's got tons of black hair!" Standing over her, I could make out nothing inside; the fact that someone had already peeked into the entranceway and seen my baby's locks made me restless to glimpse this fabled, dark-haired creature.

The last stage was surprisingly brief and anti-climactic. The doctors manipulated the forceps inside Cheryl, who pushed with all her might. Then I saw the black head come out, followed by a ruddy squirming body. Baby howled, angry and shocked to find herself airborne in such a place. It was such a relief I began to cry. Then I shook with laughter. All that anguish and grief and triumph just to extract a writhing jumbo shrimp—it was comic.

The doctor passed the newborn to her mother for inspection. She was (I may say objectively) very pretty: looked like a little Eskimo or Mexican babe, with her mop of black hair and squinting eyes. Something definitely Third World about her. An overgrown head on a scrawny trunk, she reversed her mother's disproportions. A kiss from Cheryl, then she was taken off to the side of the room and laid on a weighing table (7 pounds, 4 ounces) and given an Apgar inspection by Jackie, under a heat lamp. Lily Elena Francesca Lopate had all her fingers and toes, all her limbs, and obviously sound vocal chords. She sobbed like a whippoorwill, then brayed in and out like an affronted donkey.

Abandoned. For, while Cheryl was being stitched up by Dr. Schiller (who suddenly seemed to us to be the best doctor in the world), Lily, the jewel, the prize, the cause of all this tumult, lay on the table, crying alone. I was too intimidated by hospital procedure to go over there and comfort her, and Cheryl obviously couldn't move, and Jackie had momentarily left the room. So Lily learned right away how fickle is the world's attention.

Dr. Schiller told Cheryl she would probably have hemorrhoids for awhile, as a result of the episiotomy. Cheryl seemed glad enough that she had not died on the table. She had done her job, delivered up safely the nugget inside her. I admired her courage beyond anything I had ever seen.

Happy, relieved, physically wrung out: These were the initial reactions. For hours (I realized after the fact) I had been completely caught up in the struggle of labor, with no space left over for self-division. But that may have had more to do with the physically demanding nature of assisting a birth than with any "transcendental" wonderment about it. In fact it was less spiritually uplifting than something like boot camp. I felt as if I had gone through combat.

That night, home from the hospital, I noted in my diary all I could recall. Consulting that entry for this account, I see how blurred my understanding was—remains—by the minutiae of medical narrative. What does it all "mean," exactly? On the one hand, an experience so shocking and strange; on the other hand, so typical, so stupifyingly ordinary.

When people say that mothers don't "remember" the pain of labor, I think they mean that of course they remember, but the fact of the pain recedes next to the blessing of the child's presence on earth.

Odd: What I remember most clearly from that long night and day is the agitated *pas de deux* between Cheryl and me, holding ourselves up like marathon dancers, she cross at me for not getting her ice fast enough, me vexed at her for not appreciating that I was doing my best. Do I hold on to that memory because I can't take in the enormity of seeing a newborn burst onto the plane of existence, and so cut it down to the more mundane pattern of a couple's argument? Or is it because the tension between Cheryl and me that night pointed to a larger truth: that a woman giving birth finds herself inconsolably isolated? Close as we normally were, she had entered an experience into which I could not follow her; the promise of marriage—that we would both remain psychically connected—was of necessity broken.

I remember Cheryl sitting up, half an hour after Lily was born, still trembling and shaking.

"That's natural, for the trembling to last awhile," said Dr. Schiller.

Weeks afterward, smiling and accepting congratulations, I continued to tremble from the violence of the baby's birth. In a way, I am still trembling from it. The only comparison that comes to mind, strangely enough, is when I was mugged in the street, and I felt a tremor looking over my shoulder, for months afterward. That time my back was violated by a knife; this time I watched Cheryl's body ripped apart by natural forces, and it was almost as if it was happening to me. I am inclined to say I envied her and wanted it to be happening to me — to feel that intense an agony, for once — but that would be a lie, because at the time, not for one second did I wish I were in Cheryl's place. Orthodox Jews are taken to task for their daily prayer, "Thank God I am not a woman." And they should be criticized, since it is a crude, chauvinistic thought; but it is also an understandable one in certain situations, and I found myself viscerally "praying" something like that, while trying to assist Cheryl in her pushes.

Thank God I am not someone else. Thank God I am only who I am. These are the thoughts that simultaneously create and imprison the self. If ego is a poisonous disease (and it is), it is one I unfortunately trust more than its cure. I began as a detached skeptic and was shoved by the long night into an un-willing empathy, which saw Cheryl as a part of me, or me of her, for maybe a hundred seconds in all, before returning to a more self-protective distance. Detachment stands midway between two poles: at one end, solipsism; at the other end, wisdom. Those of us who are only halfway to wisdom know how close we still lean toward the chillness of solipsism.

It is too early to speak of Lily. This charming young lady, willful, passionate and insisting on engagement on her terms, who has already taught me more about unguarded love and the dread meaning of responsibility than I ever hoped to learn, may finally convince me there are other human beings as real as myself.

Child of the Sun — Gabriel's Birth (Sun Prayer)

JIMMY SANTIAGO BACA

to Gabriel

Beatrice on the bed, muscles twitch pain,
  "No, uh, the pain. . . ."
Marsha offers warm wet towel,
   "No, no, no, it's too painful. . . ."
Beatrice paces bedroom, cross corn-planting blanket,
   barefoot through rows of Corn Dancers,
caressing abdomen, deep breathing,
lips expelling flurries of pain,
while her fingers circle belly-button,
trying to ease the pain.
  In a tub of warm water,
  Beatrice rises,
   "O, uhh, no," pulls my hands into hers.
We stand together in the bathroom,
window sunlight at her back
silhouettes her body
to a shadow sunlight smolders off of.
She radiates light streams,
her face grimaces intense pain and pleasure,
her head lolls forward, her long black hair
veils my face
as I kneel before her on the bathroom floor, and say,
"Prop your right leg on the toilet seat,
that's it, now push, push, sweetheart. . . ."
Through vines of hair I peer,
between her spread legs, where blinding light
streams through. Our dark bodies
create a cave dwelling, entered through hair.

She mutters grunted pleas,
aggressive throaty squeals,
grips my shoulders,
her warm breath pants at my head,
her body,
drips sweat onto mine.
Sunlight radiates
through wild roses and green vines
that press against the window
at her back,
and rages between her legs.
She gives a half-choked sob
and upside down
suspended between her legs
surfacing from sunlight,
leaves and flowers,
a thousand-year-old face appears,
Gabriel! Gabriel!
Flying dark shape in sunlight,
God descending from sky
upside down
between woman's legs,
arms and face glisten darkly with uterine juice,
shimmery,
it wriggles free of mother skin,
fierce glum godhead stone face
I stare at through vine hair,
its dark eyes squinch-lidded
unwrinkle wide in haunting ferocity
at me,
and instantly I am tossed,
from my body into a wheel of sunlight,
disembodied

in sheer blaze of dazzling lightwaves,
I am hurled
like a spark from my chimney-flue body
on an updraft of his presence —

Gabriel slips from her trembling loins,
filmy with juice,
thick rivulets of blood
run down our hands, arms, wrists,
into my hands,
cries angrily at me,
and I brush through vines of hair,
rise in blue sunlight haze
misting the bathroom,
and offer Gabriel, child of the Sun,
to Beatrice,
then look at the window
and bow to the sunlight,
for our child's safe arrival.

Birth Report

STEPHEN DOBYNS

The week the nuclear protesters stormed the gates
of the Seabrook plant was the same week you were born.
The protesters were repelled. You spent thirty hours
being forced from your mother's body, while I filled
sheets of yellow paper charting the length of each pain.
The week of the first snow was the week you were born.
The week the Pope packed Yankee Stadium. The week of the first
stories of people freezing to death due to the cost of oil.
In bright light, I watched your head ease itself out of
my wife's vagina: your scalp blue, flecked with blood.
The week of the World Series and new boredoms on television.
The week politicians maneuvered election year mileage
out of Russian troops in Cuba. The week a racist
from Philadelphia gave me three dollars for your
future and warned you to stay out of Philadelphia.
I took you and bathed you in a plastic tub in the first
seconds of your life, while you twisted and cried; and
outside the world lunged and snapped at the hospital door,
and trees turned color; and corporate business tried
to make certain you would inherit the small change;
and governments arranged a little war for when you got
older; and friends, relatives, even strangers wished you
many fine years on the muckheap, as they pursued their
blindfolded, arms-folded lives and politely helped
each other into the oven. And everybody promised you
your own place in the oven, your own meat hook,
your own hole in the head, own hole in the ground,

as they shut down their brains to the destruction
and stultifying boredom and once more decided
to keep their money on the big promise: the spirit
of this country rising out of the east like a great
red mouth — tearing and rending, devouring its children.

Waiting

LISA LENZO

I shift my weight on the high hospital bed, take a quick, deep breath, and let it out like steam. Ray looks up. "How are you doing?" he asks. He's sitting across the room on a blue plastic chair, a tan lunch tray abandoned on his knees.

"I'm doing fine," I say, meeting Ray's gaze, trying to gauge how he's feeling. But it's as if he's a lover I haven't yet learned to read. "Come check out your kid," I say. "He's moving just a little — stretching, I think." Ray sets aside the lunch tray and walks over to the bed. During my first pregnancy, Ray would rest his hands on my belly, he would press his cheek close, and also his lips. But now Ray only touches my belly with his fingers, and his touch is light, and his smile is like a ghost's.

Ray returns to his chair, and I look at the VCR screen, at a tape on breast-feeding that a nurse has put in. Filling the screen is a softly smiling mother and her nursing, contented child; the baby is alert, gazing into its mother's eyes.

Dr. Cal reappears in the doorway and says, "Annie? Ray? We can have an operating room at two-thirty. How would you like to meet your baby half an hour from now?" Ray and I nod and smile. All three of us are grinning as if we're about to open some big gift; inside me, where the gift lies, a contraction begins. It feels as if a giant hand is spreading there, thrusting outward through all my flesh, the huge fingers pressing too hard, threatening to hurt me badly, but holding back for now. The threat of worse to come makes me think of the last time I gave birth, and it's as if a shark has risen into sunny water, swimming up from lightless depths. Dr. Cal and Ray don't seem aware of the threat right now. Maybe they're just pretending to be oblivious of it. I keep smiling, pretending to be oblivious, too. But I remind myself not to get too happy, that there's power here far beyond our control.

Dr. Cal leaves the room, taking Ray with him, and two green-clothed women walk in and get to work. They help me into a gown, insert an IV needle into my right hand, tape that hand and arm to an IV board, and strap the board to the bed. "You ladies move fast," I say, trying to get them to look at me. "I feel like I'm at a car wash." The women smile but don't meet my eyes; they're too busy. They shift their hands to the base of my big belly and wash and then shave the top of my pubic hair, where the incision will be made. The scar from the last time is still noticeable. The knife will enter at the same place.

But this will not be like the last time, I'm almost sure, although we are at greater risk.

Ray and I haven't talked much about it. It's as if we're on separate boats heading for the same shore. I'm holding my boat steady, Ray's holding his. It's all that we can do for now, almost more than we can do. Later we'll meet up again, when this is all over. Meanwhile our boats surround us like empty shells. Dr. Cal flutters above our bows like a bird and flies ahead toward where the shore will be, if it is there.

The two green-clothed women drape a sheet over my outstretched legs and big belly and tuck it tightly all around so I can't move. But I tell them to leave my left arm free—I want it to hold the baby—and they do as I say, they leave my arm unrestrained and outside the sheet. Last time both of my arms were tied down, and they took the baby away without letting me see her. This time everything will be different, I tell myself again, and I think of the child I dreamed.

He was sitting on my kitchen counter with red sunlight washing over him. The light rippled like water, its redness turning him pink. He was sitting up by himself. He looked healthy and strong. I woke up feeling someone had made me a promise. My promise dream, I call it in my head, my true dream, even though I don't always believe in it.

When I told the dream to Ray, lying beside him in bed, Ray didn't say anything. I could feel him holding himself somewhere far off. We've lived together for five years, since we were twenty-one and eighteen, but it's felt to me this past year as if we've been living apart.

Last fall, two months after the birth, we took a trip to Isle Royale, a gift from my parents intended to give us solace and time alone together to help us regroup. My parents arranged for lodging and meals for a week, but Ray and I left at the end of the third day. To me, each day on the island felt seamed in by sadness, a pouch of sadness that enclosed all the land, lake, and sky, but I felt better there than I did at home. Still, nothing I said could convince Ray to stay. As soon as we reached the island, my menstrual cycle resumed, and Ray was afraid I might be pregnant again and miscarrying. I tried to assure Ray that I was all right, but Ray didn't trust my judgment or our luck. He felt panicky, he said. Even if I weren't miscarrying, so many other things could go wrong, with me or with him. Anything could happen, and the nearest hospital was half an hour away by plane. I pointed out that we had been far more isolated four years ago while backpacking in British Columbia, but Ray only said, "Yes, I know that. I didn't realize the risk we were taking."

The green-clothed women finish their prep work, and an orderly wheels me to the elevator and takes me down to the basement, leaving me by myself in a windowless hall. All I have to do now is wait. I've already waited nine months, plus the nine months of my other pregnancy, and the three months between; a few more minutes will be easy, I think.

As if to contradict me, a contraction begins, the same huge hand stretching and probing now, pressing too hard. The hand feels vicious, as if it wants to hurt me and also to test me, to see how much stirring up, how much messing with I can take. It makes me think of the hand of a torturer, and I wonder how such a feeling of evil can be part of the beginning of life. I think of the child I dreamed, and now that pink light washing over his skin makes me think of water tinted with blood. I think of that pink, bloody light covering my child and make myself stop. I decided at the beginning of this pregnancy that I wouldn't cry any more, and for the past nine months I've managed to keep myself steady. Just wait, I remind myself now, looking around at the brown basement walls, the pipes running along them up near the ceiling. It's so quiet down here, buried beneath the earth, as if the surgeons chose this place to help them with cutting downward and inward.

Another pair of green-clothed women appear on either side of my cart. The taller one touches my strapped right hand, checking the IV tube; the other one lifts my free left arm, holding it up for the taller one to see. "Oh, that should have been restrained," the taller woman says.

I want to pull my arm away, but there's nowhere to hide it. The short woman starts to tie a strap around my wrist. "Don't," I say. "My doctor said I could have it free."

"We're tying it loosely, see?" the tall blond woman answers.

"I can't have it tied at all," I say. "I'm going to use it to hold the baby after he's born."

The short woman hesitates; she doesn't knot the cloth.

"You're not going to hold your baby anyway," the tall woman says, not realizing the threat in her words. Again I feel the shark swim up, the water turning nightmare black. "Caesarean babies are taken immediately to the nursery," the tall woman explains. "And if your arm isn't restrained during the operation, you might contaminate the sterile field. You don't want to contaminate the sterile field, do you?"

"I'm not going to," I say. "I'm —"

"Well then it has to be tied."

The tall woman and I continue to argue, in level voices. The woman keeps asking me if I want to contaminate the sterile field; I keep telling her that I'm going to keep my arm out of the way of the operation and that I have my doctor's permission to have my arm free.

We've drawn an audience of green-clothed people: six or seven of them stand in a loose half-circle around my cart. I know that my arm will have to be untied before the operation so that the anesthetist can inject the spinal, but I'm afraid that once I'm tied down, though they'll free me for a moment, they'll tie me right up again afterward. With the last birth, that's how it went, in rapid steps — no, in leaps — from a natural birth, to a standard Caesarean, to being knocked out without my permission or even my knowledge, to never seeing my baby at all.

Finally the tall woman says, "Well, you can talk it over with your doctor when you see him. For now that arm is going to have to be tied." The short woman knots the strap, and the green-clothed onlookers look disappointed. Everyone walks away. I lift my arm like a dog testing its leash. There are three inches of strap between my wrist and the bed rail. My other arm, taped to the IV board and strapped to the other rail, is completely immobile, as are my legs, belly, and feet, bound by the deeply tucked sheets. The hand inside me tightens into a fist, then spreads its fingers and digs, and digs deeper. Again I feel the shark. He's so close I can't tell where he is.

I'm wheeled to the operating room, where a fat, fair-skinned nurse and a dark, wiry anesthetist are waiting for me. The nurse untucks the sheets and methodically unties the arm that the other women and I just made such a fuss over. Then the nurse and the anesthetist help me onto my side. "Do your best to get into a fetal position," the nurse says.

I curl around my big belly and close my eyes tight, and the anesthetist walks his fingers down my spine, feeling for a good place to insert the needle. A cold wet spot appears on my back, and I smell alcohol. "So," the anesthetist says in a chatty voice, "how many children do you have at home?"

I feel as if I've been struck. I lose my breath. Then my body convulses, and I can't hold back my sobs.

I can sense the nurse and the anesthetist beyond the wall of my crying, beyond my heaving body; they're waiting for me to stop, or to explain myself, or for a clue about what they can do. I know that they must have a good idea of why I'm crying, but suddenly I need to tell them; I can hardly speak, but I want to pull the truth out of the dark. The words come out of me in pieces: "My — one — baby — died."

I don't realize that I've been gone until I come back, to the sound of my crying, and the weight of two soft hands pressing my shoulder and my hip, and two leaner, harder hands resting against my back and the back of my neck. It feels as if they're holding me together.

The nurse suggests I try breathing deeply and slowly, and I try it and it works. It's as if I'm learning to breathe for the first time; all I hear and feel is my own breath as it leaves and enters my body. "Okay," I say. "I'm ready now."

Again I curl in on myself as far as I'm able. The anesthetist fingers my spine, and the cool wet spot reappears. "Hold perfectly still now," he says. There's a pause, an absolute stillness.

I don't feel the needle going in, but the anesthetist says "Finished," and he and the nurse help me onto my back. The nurse reties the arm strap quickly, unthinkingly, as if she were retying a shoe. Then she goes to the door and lets in a group of green-clothed people, among them Ray and Dr. Cal.

As soon as all of them have taken their places, I raise my left arm the few inches the strap allows. "Can I have this arm free?" I ask, looking into Dr. Cal's eyes, the only part of him not hidden by cloth.

Dr. Cal looks over my head, and I can tell that his friendly, piercing gaze is looking right into the anesthetist. "What do you say, Doctor?" Dr. Cal says. "You're never going to get a better patient."

This might be a lie. I don't know how I'll react. Dr. Cal wasn't at the last birth. The doctor who was knocked me out seconds afterward, before I could suspect that something was wrong.

The anesthetist must nod or shrug his agreement. Dr. Cal picks up my wrist, and, with a scalpel that has appeared in his hand like magic, he slices the strap in two with one stroke. I take Ray's hand in mine and face the cloth screen rising above me and the table. Now things will move fast. Now the waiting is as close as it can be to being over.

A scalpel stings across me like a fingernail tracing a line; then the whole inside of my belly is moving as if the baby is wrestling with the doctor's hands. It doesn't hurt, but it's frightening; it feels too powerful, more than my body can bear. Then a sudden, tremendous absence exists, as if someone has knocked me hollow.

"It's a girl," someone says; *a girl*, I think, and before I can ask to see her, she is being held above me. Her skin is a bright, deep blue, the way the sky gets sometimes in fall, on the clearest, most brilliant of days. I can see right away that she's healthy and strong. Ray sees it, too; he says into my ear, "She looks good, Annie, she looks really good."

The baby is twisting and struggling in the doctor's hands, crying and fighting the bulb syringe suctioning liquid from her mouth. The bulb syringe follows her struggling head, and she twists the other way, breaking free.

Beneath the baby's crying, I notice a strange sound, coming from somewhere close. It's a sound like I've never heard, human and inhuman, stranger than the blueness of my daughter's skin. I listen to it with no idea of what it is until I realize that it's coming from me: a low, keening moan; sad, hopeless, inconsolable; but what makes it so strange is that it isn't sustained — it starts and it stops, broken by my laughter.

My baby stops crying and is placed in my arm. She's breathing deeply and beginning to turn pink; pink is overtaking the blue, starting from the center of her chest and spreading outward, washing over her like water, like light.

Ancestral Lights

DEBORAH DIGGES

I love to go to the light section
of big department stores among huge
table lamps and cheap chandeliers,
all of them ablaze, the walls mirrors.
Here an aging human face confronts
the present tense, its dead brilliance.
In the long refraction I'm first in line,
the ancestors eclipsed in the dark under my eyes,
in the sharp, angular nose shadows,
as once, transfigured onto passports, called
into the literal translation of a name at Ellis Island,
I was a new moon in their fingerprints.
And summer nights under the stars
as my father sang us *The Ninety and Nine,*
I rejoiced with the angels for the lost sheep found.
I thought great cries went up in heaven.
I'd never know how many blood redemptions
it had taken, how many lifetimes,
simply to lie there, whole, myself, safe
in the coarsening grass of a Missouri August.
Then I believed in everything.
I wept openly before the bright lights flooding
the congregation, as if eternity could live in me
like the accidental star inside the apple,
like the apple, however blighted, inside the tree.

They say the one thing we remember always
is faces, each one moored to the senses
so that by death we host a multitude
who wear the farewell garments
in which they've seemed to us most themselves —
as my brothers will wave to me in their dirty
work clothes smelling of creosote and apples,
and my sisters, among the lilacs,
in bright colored summer dresses like my own.
And though I know now that heaven may be
only the mind's fear of the wonders it imagines,
the way our best thoughts surprise us
and seem not to be our own, I like to believe
we turn into light around those we love,
or would have loved, had we known them,
and warn them through the blood
by ringing in their ears.
Just after the birth of my first son,
when I tried to sit up too quickly to hold him,
I saw a thousand secret stars spray the delivery room,
and linger, and rise upward,
as if all the failures of my people
had ignited there in greeting
and through the life of this child now
could continue their long healing.

The First Day

ELIZABETH SPIRES

The ward is quiet, the mothers delivered,
except in one a woman labors still and calls,
with a sharp cry, that she is dying.
She is not dying but cannot know it now.
Trapped in the birthstorm, I did not cry,
but saw my body as the enemy
I could not accommodate, could not deny.
Morning arrived, and my daughter.
That's how it is in this world, birth, death,
matter-of-fact, happening like that.
The room was warm. The room was full of flowers,
her face all petals and leaves, a flower
resembling such as I had never seen.
All day she slept beside me, eyes darting
beneath bruised blue eyelids, retracing the journey,
dreaming the birth dream over and over
until it held no fear for her.
I dared not wake her. The hours passed.
I rested as her soul poured in her body,
the way clear water, poured from a height,
takes the shape of a flaring vase or glass, or light
fills a room's corners on a brilliant winter morning.
Slowly, she opened her eyes, a second waking,
taking me by surprise, a bright being
peering out from behind dark eyes,
as if she already knew what sights would be seen,

what marvels lay ahead of her, weariness and woe,
the joists and beams, the underpinnings of the world
shifting a little to make room for her.
The first day was over forever. Tranced,
I picked up the pen, the paper, and wrote:
I have had a child. Now I must live with death.

How It Begins

DAVID MURA

Those first hours, that first day, the late winter light lengthening shadows in
    the room
— "Samantha," I said, looking out on flurries, spontaneously naming her,
"the day you were born was a grey and blustery day" —
Visitors coming and going, night feedings when the ghostly nurses entered,
padding about in the dark, bearing this bundle . . . And as her infant
    metabolic energies,
her untethered desires, still seemed to reside in that globally aquatic, belly
    buried nook,
its muffled thumps, all entrancing dark, pops, hisses, distant and near with
    echoing voices,
so holding her in your arms, watching her tongue slip in, slip out, that tiny
    glistening hole,
center now of your world, desire tethered again, back to the mother,
the pumping arteries and thump of the chest, the liquid stream and gnawing
    gums,
suck and slurp and swallow of flesh, her eyes drifting upwards to your face,
rolling in some drunken blissed-out ecstasy which *you* half feared — after all,
what were those years of medical training for? — was a sign of incipient
    epileptic attack:
so you, still deep in aftermath, peace which flooded her coming with the
    blood of paradise,
turned and whispered, "I feel like Demeter, like I've gone after her, into this
    dark underworld cavern;
later on we'll both come up into the noise of this world. . . ."

Holding Bernadette

HUNT HAWKINS

In a room without windows, my infant daughter
struggles in the underwater
glow of the bilirubin light.
She clutches my finger, opens muddy eyes,
and gives me a puzzled look.
The machines blink and sing. I have no answers.
Even with three tubes, she can't
get enough glucose. I feel ashamed
for all the gray mornings driving to work
when I've half-wished to get it over.
I tell her we'll go fishing,
then explain how fish are funny, slippery animals
who live in the Gulf, miles away.
Her stupid heart! It thinks it can save itself
by cutting off circulation to her limbs.
I want to save myself by turning away,
but Elaine insists we return at midnight
to hold Bernadette.
How could the pioneers have toiled across the plains,
leaving child after child under empty stones?
She breathes softly, holding on,
her heart beating with its savage wish.
I want to tell her
how I felt at home once
in a tent west of Morogoro in Africa.

Waking in late afternoon,
I saw far away across the savannah
a family of giraffes moving in golden light
with their awkward, watery gait.
The grass billowed so peacefully,
as if holding all the generations.
In the parking garage
Elaine and I look at each other.
What is there to say?
Beneath her blouse her breasts are bound
to stop the milk.

Milk

How many nurses cared for her needs? The first dressed Bea's wound, a puckered red mouth silenced with staples. A second nurse brought her a cup of chilled juice to wash away the sour taste in her mouth. A third nurse, a man, massaged her sore back.

Then a fourth nurse came in, a small dark-haired woman with a pen in her curls. She knelt beside Bea's bed and covered her feet with paper slippers, then helped Bea to stand and shuffle to the bathroom. Bea's bladder was bursting, but everything below her waist was so numb nothing came out. When she finally gave up, the toilet bowl was gory with blood and clots of tissue. Had a mess like this really come from her body? Even as she stood there, blood dripped to the floor. She bent to wipe it up and nearly passed out. Too embarrassed to ask the nurse to do this for her, she left the blood on the tiles. The nurse handed her a belt and a sanitary napkin as thick as a book, then helped Bea lie down.

"If you need anything at all pull that cord by your bed and ask for Patrice." The nurse tapped a pill into Bea's palm. "Do you want your baby?" she said.

She was asking, of course, if Bea wanted to see him. But the question Bea heard was: Do you want to keep the baby you've just given birth to?

She hadn't conceived him on purpose. She had slept with a man without taking precautions, like any ignorant schoolgirl. But she had decided to keep him. She had worked with abstractions for so many years she had forgotten it was possible to sometimes catch a glimpse of the thing in itself. When she realized that a fetus was growing in the universe deep in her womb, she couldn't bear to abort it. She talked to it for months, asking it questions. She looked forward to meeting it as she would have looked forward to meeting an alien who could tell her what life on another planet was like. But for now she was tired. She swallowed the pill, then slept like a woman who has been up for three days and has just given birth to an eleven-pound child.

She awoke to a gong. Cheering. Applause. A floor-length blue curtain surrounded her bed. From beyond it came the sounds of a television turned up full volume.

An orderly brought soup. The warm salty broth tasted so delicious Bea savored each sip. Then she turned to watch the sun set above the river; the buildings dissolved until only the lights in their windows were visible. A distant observer would have guessed that the city was nothing more substantial than a few panes of glass with light bulbs behind, as earthly astronomers had assumed for so long that the universe was made of comets and stars, of things they could see. Instead, it turned out that all but a fraction of the cosmos was dark, invisible matter — black holes, some new gas, giant cold planets.

Bea looked around, as if someone could see her thinking about invisible matter instead of her child. She heard her roommate say: "Lie still, stop your wiggling." Bea was certain that if only she could watch another mother diaper her baby she would learn to do this herself, but the heavy blue curtain blocked her roommate from view.

In fact, Bea didn't see her roommate until late that afternoon, though the woman's TV was on the whole time — soap operas, game shows, even cartoons. Every so often the woman groaned. Then, about four, the curtain rings squealed and Bea's roommate emerged. She was short, but so broad that her johnny wouldn't close, exposing a dark swatch of buttocks and spine. She was thirty, maybe older, her hair short and shapeless. Crooked in one arm was a half-naked child; in the other hand, a diaper. She scuffed to the bathroom in her blue paper slippers without glancing at Bea. After ten or fifteen minutes, she opened the door and scuffed beyond the curtain.

When Bea hobbled to the bathroom to use the toilet herself, she saw a mustardy smear on the lid of the trash can. Why hadn't the woman wiped up her baby's feces? Well, maybe some people just weren't clean. This thought upset her, of course. Wasn't it more logical that her roommate simply hadn't noticed the dirt? Or she still was too weak to juggle a baby and a wet paper towel? Probably, she had left the smear where it was in the confidence that the janitor would wipe it away. The next time he came, though, he left the smear on the can, and the stain of Bea's blood on the tiles near the bowl.

The nurse rolled a Plexiglas crib through the curtain. The baby inside was swaddled in blankets. His eyes were screwed tight but his mouth was wide open, like the mouth of a pitcher waiting for someone to fill it with milk.

"He's hungry," Patrice said. She lay the child in Bea's lap, across her incision.

This is my son, Bea repeated to herself, over and over, but the fact seemed unreal. He was fair, she was dark. He was heavy and round, with a triple chin and jowls, she was gaunt, with high cheekbones. (Did he look like his father? She could barely recall.)

"What's his name?" Patrice asked.

"Isaac," Bea told her, and, as she named him, he suddenly seemed real.

"Isaac," Patrice repeated. "Biblical names are so full of meaning."

Bea didn't bother to explain that she had named her son after Sir Isaac Newton.

"Time to get started," Patrice said. "Your milk won't come in until tomorrow, at least, but you both need the practice."

Bea weighed a breast in one palm: it felt like a Baggie with a spoonful of milk in the bottom. She lifted her son. He was crying from hunger but wouldn't turn his head to suck.

"Here's the trick," Patrice said. Gripping Bea's nipple, she rubbed it across the baby's cheek.

As if by arrangement, Isaac turned toward the nipple and opened his mouth. When he clamped down his gums the pain was so intense that Bea cried out and jerked back. He was wailing more shrilly. She let him latch on again, steeling herself not to push him away. The pain slowly abated. Still, as he sucked, she felt a vague irritation, as if a street corner beggar kept pulling at her arm.

"That's enough," Patrice said, just as Bea started to feel more at ease. "I'll take him to the nursery. Here's a pamphlet to study." The cover showed a mother in a lacy white nightgown smiling down at an infant nuzzling her breast. "A bruiser like this will want to eat every hour," Patrice said. "He'll be an eating machine. You've got to relax!"

It was after eleven but Bea couldn't sleep. In another few days she would have to take her child home. She had never been alone with a baby. Her mother lived in Cleveland and was legally blind. Few of her friends or colleagues had children. She had read books about babies, but she sensed that a new kind of knowledge was called for.

Still, she might be able to fall asleep, if only her roommate would turn off her TV. Bea hated to ask, but if she did so politely, pleading the strains of their common ordeal . . . She crossed the room, barefoot, and nudged aside the curtain.

The woman sat with her knees drawn to her chest, her baby propped against her shins. She was watching a talk show whose dapper black host Bea knew she should recognize. He said something about a basketball player named Larry and the woman snorted through her nose.

"I didn't mean to disturb you. It's just, well, it's late."

The woman seemed to expect that Bea would do what she had to — take her pulse or draw blood — and leave her alone. She stared at the screen with such a fierce gravity that no light leaked out.

"Your baby," Bea said, just to make herself known. But then, to determine what to say next, she had to look at the child. It wore a frilly pink dress. Thick auburn hair curled past its ears. Its coppery brown skin was lustrous and smooth. "She's pretty," Bea said.

"Huh. That child ain't no she." The woman seemed to say this without moving her lips. Bea needed to shut her eyes to concentrate on what her roommate was saying.

"Oh, I'm sorry. I didn't—"

"Ain't your fault. Didn't I buy all these dresses? How's anyone supposed to know a baby's a boy if he's wearing a dress?"

The thought crossed Bea's mind that only a poor, uneducated woman would predict her baby's sex based on old wives' tales. "You thought you'd have a girl?"

"'Thought' nothing. Those doctors took a picture with that sound thing, said they couldn't see no johnson, I had me a girl."

Bea felt suddenly ashamed, as she did when a colleague found a mistake in a paper she had written. The baby started to fuss. Though his mother's huge breasts swelled beneath her johnny and were ringed with wet cloth, she poked a bottle in his mouth. Bea almost believed the woman did this to spite her. "What's his name?" she asked.

"Only name he's got is fit for a girl. Can't think of no new name until I ask his father. Man don't like it, his boy gets some name he ain't said he liked."

Bea couldn't help but think that a man who cared so much about his son's name ought to have attended the baby's birth. "Did you have a Caesarean?" She asked this for reasons she didn't like to admit: if the woman said no, she might leave the next day and be replaced by a roommate who wouldn't make Bea feel so self-conscious or watch TV all the time. "Or was it natural?" she said, to mask her suspicion that the woman didn't know what "Caesarean" meant.

"'Natural,' huh. Last time I was in here I had me twin girls. Doctors cut my belly open, I went home in two days. This time I had this teensy little boy, came out on his own the minute I got here, no cutting, no drugs, I can barely stand up. Hurts me down there like a sonofabitch."

The woman pushed the buttons on her remote until she found the news. A snowstorm. A plane crash. The mayor of Washington had just been arrested for buying cocaine. According to his lawyer, the mayor had been framed by government officials waging a vendetta against powerful blacks.

"Huh." The woman faced Bea. "What you think? Think he's guilty?"

Did Bea? Of course. "He's innocent until they prove he isn't," she said.

Whatever the test she had been given, she had failed it. The woman rolled toward the curtain, her backside toward Bea and her fleshy black forearm shielding her son. Then she seemed to fall asleep as a movie about the attack on Pearl Harbor unrolled its credits over Bea's head.

Someone was jiggling Bea's leg.

"I'm sorry," Patrice said, "but you'll have to get used to it." Patrice handed her Isaac. He was crying again. "I don't want to worry you, but if you can't feed him soon we'll have to give him formula. Then he won't want to suck. And if that happens, well, your milk will never come in."

His mouth worked her nipple. Where was this milk supposed to come from? Bea wondered. Why couldn't she simply will it to be?

The baby sucked at each side for exactly eight minutes; Patrice timed him, eyes trained on the watch on her sharply cocked wrist.

"You don't have to do that," Bea said. She heard an unfamiliar edge in her voice.

The nurse stopped and stood blinking. She picked at the beads trimming her sweater as if these were burrs. It occurred to Bea then that Patrice was as uncomfortable with people as she was. Unlike the other nurses, Patrice couldn't seem to sense what a patient might want. Bea pitied her for being so poorly suited to the job she had chosen, as she pitied the student who had been her advisee for the past seven years; he thought that *having vision* meant seeing stars clearly through a telescope.

Patrice stopped picking at her sweater. "Never mind," she said. "I can be that way sometimes. We'll try again tomorrow." She wheeled the crib toward the door. Beyond the blue curtain she said to Bea's roommate: "Wake up there. Wake up. Don't you know you could crush her? Here, let me take her back to the nursery."

"Uh-uh. You leave that baby right where he is. I don't want my baby in no nursery."

Bea wondered if her roommate really believed that the nurses would purposely try to harm her son. She was being . . . what was the word? *Paranoid*, Bea thought, then she managed to fall asleep.

It was just after breakfast. A girl with red hair poked her face through the curtain. "Statistics," she said. She consulted her clipboard. "Are you Beatrice Weller?"

Bea nodded.

"Maiden name?"

"Beatrice Weller."

The girl regarded Bea closely. She asked what Bea "did."

"I'm a cosmologist," Bea said. She started to explain that cosmologists were scientists who studied the universe—how it formed, how it grew. But the girl interrupted.

"You do makeup? And hair?"

Bea surprised herself by saying, "Um. Sure."

"Do you mind if I ask how much you charge for making someone over? Before, you know, and after? Could you maybe do me?"

"Oh, no," Bea said. "I couldn't. I don't have my . . . tools."

The girl seemed disappointed. "Are you sure? It's important. I mean, there's this guy I just met. You'll think I'm silly, but maybe, I don't know, you could give me some beauty tips? I get paid Wednesday morning." She leaned forward, head cocked, her palms pressed together.

"Well. I suppose. I'll be here until Friday." She would think of something later. Already she sensed that, once you began, it was easy to say things you didn't mean.

"Oh, thanks!" the girl said. She asked a few last questions: Bea's nationality (U.S.) and her age (thirty-six). "I'm sure you had the sense not to smoke or use drugs while you were pregnant." She made a mark on a form, promised to return for her beauty consultation, then dragged a chair behind the curtain. "Hello? Coreen Jones?"

Since the name was so common it had the effect of making Bea's roommate seem less real, not more so, as if she weren't a person but a whole class of objects: chair, atom, Jones.

Bea couldn't help but eavesdrop. Coreen mumbled her answers, which the girl asked her to repeat again and again, her voice louder each time.

"You're unemployed?"

"No, I ain't."

"You've got a job?" the girl asked. "Where?"

"At a school."

"You've got a job at a school?"

"Don't worry," Coreen mumbled. "All I do is cook there."

And so on, until the girl asked Coreen for the name of her child.

"Ain't got one."

"Excuse me?"

"I said my baby doesn't have no name."

"She doesn't have a name?"

"It's a he, not a she, and he doesn't have a name."

Tell her, Bea thought. It isn't your fault. You're not a bad mother. But Coreen explained nothing.

The girl asked Coreen if her child had a father.

"Think I done it myself?"

"I *meant* are you married."

"Man never needed no piece of paper to make him a father."

The girl asked for his name. Coreen mumbled an answer. "Can you spell that?" the girl asked.

"Always make sure I can spell a man's name before I have his baby." Coreen spelled the letters slowly: "N . . . A . . . T . . . E." This ordeal over, the girl asked Coreen for her "ethnic category."

"American," Coreen said.

"Oh, no," said the girl, "I mean, where were you born?"

"America," Coreen said.

"Well, what country do you *come* from?"

"Come from? Way back? Guess you could say Sierra Leone."

"That's not a country. It's a mountain. In Mexico."

"Sure it's a country. Sierra Leone."

"All right then, where is it?"

"West Africa," Coreen said.

"But that's not a country! You mean *South* Africa."

Bea heard Coreen grunt. "You so smart, you put down whatever country you want. You got any more questions?"

"Only one," the girl said. "Now, try to think hard. Did you use alcohol, or smoke cigarettes, or take any drugs at all—heroin, or cocaine, or even marijuana—while your child was inside you?"

A pause. Bea was startled to hear Coreen laugh.

"Girl, if I done all that awful shit to my baby, he wouldn't have turned out so perfect, now would he."

Bea had just spent another fruitless half-hour nursing her son when a woman's harsh voice barked over the intercom that the photographer was there to take pictures of their babies, but they had to line up by the door to Room 3 within the next fifteen minutes or forfeit their chance. She usually considered taking pictures to be vulgar and vain. But if something were to happen to Isaac, she wouldn't have a picture to remember what he looked like.

From behind the blue curtain came the sounds of her roommate preparing her child. Bea took Isaac as he was, in a hospital T-shirt stamped BETH ZION, BETH ZION, as if this were his name. The two women wheeled their babies' cribs down the hall. Every few steps Coreen clutched her belly. Her forehead was wet, her face ashen.

"Are you all right?" Bea asked. "If you want, I could take him—" She was suddenly afraid Coreen would react with the same paranoia she had shown toward Patrice.

Coreen mumbled what sounded like "tell me I'm fine" and kept pushing the crib.

They lined up behind a dozen other mothers, half Coreen's age, their hair elegantly done up in beads and stiff braids. Their babies, like Coreen's, were dressed in fancy outfits; one of the boys wore suspenders and a bow tie. A middle-aged woman in a pink linen suit handed out brochures. When Bea saw the cheapest price she nearly turned back. But when would Isaac be a newborn again? She wiped the spittle from his mouth. He gnawed at her finger with sharply ridged gums.

"Huh," Coreen said. "How come they never tell you what things like this cost 'til you're standing in line?"

Bea expected her roommate to wheel her baby's crib back to their room. How could she afford twenty dollars for a picture? Bad enough she was spending an extra five dollars a day for TV, an expense Bea herself, from years of living on a stipend, had elected to save.

But Coreen stayed in line. She filled out the form, holding it against the back of the woman in front of her. She let the photographer perch her son on a pillow and snap a light in his face.

"I'm not buying it right now," she told the woman in pink. "But you better take good care of it. That boy's bound to be famous. Reporters need his picture, you just might be rich."

Bea hadn't wanted anyone to see her until she had gotten the hang of taking care of her son. She disconnected the phone, but in the middle of the week a boy in a Mohawk brought her a towering basket of fruit. "Congratulations on your own Little Bang!" read the card, "from the crew." Her friend Modhumita, who worked in a lab not far from the hospital, stopped by every day. Bea caught herself hoping that her roommate would see Mita's dusky brown skin and think she was black.

Coreen's phone rang often, but no one came to visit. From what Bea could tell, none of Coreen's friends could get time off from work, or they couldn't leave their children. As the TV set blared, Coreen told a friend what she hadn't told Bea.

Her "pains" had begun on the subway to work. "Know what scared is?" she said. "Scared's thinking you're gonna drop your baby right there on that nasty old floor, all those white boys looking up your nookie."

Instead of getting off at the stop near the school, Coreen took the train to her clinic. "Time I get inside I can't hardly walk, they say I'm still closed, I got a month to go, it's only false pains. I say, 'You ain't careful, you gonna have yourself a false little baby right there in your lap,' but they don't want to hear it. I go out and call Lena and ask could she keep the twins a while longer. Then I call me an ambulance. Time it pulls up, driver says, 'How come you people always waiting 'til the last minute? You like giving birth to your babies outdoors?'"

Her friend must have asked a question.

"Nate?" Coreen said. "He's away on some haul, don't even know yet." She complained she didn't feel well; she was all hot and cold and she "hurt something awful." Then she shushed whoever was on the other end because the announcer was saying that the police had a videotape of Marion Barry smoking cocaine in that Washington hotel room, and not with his wife.

"Huh," Coreen said. "They got his black ass by the balls. Just let him try to lie now."

After dinner that night Patrice brought in Isaac. He worked Bea's nipples so hard he raised a welt on his lip, but still no milk came.

"He's losing weight," Patrice told her. "You'll have to calm down. Just look at his face and think loving thoughts."

But the baby kept crying. His face was red as lava; his mouth might have been a crater into which Bea had been ordered to leap. According to Patrice, if Bea's milk didn't come in within twenty-four hours they would have to give him formula.

"Hey!" Coreen called. "I need me a doctor."

Patrice shot Bea a glance, then flung the curtain aside. "You're just engorged," she said. "That means your breasts are too full. We'll have to dry you up. Then you'll feel better."

Bea wondered why her roommate wasn't nursing her child. Didn't she know that it was healthier and cheaper to breastfeed? Maybe she disliked the feel of a mouth tugging at her nipple as much as Bea herself did. Or perhaps she couldn't afford to stay home with the baby. Bea stared at the curtain. Why could she imagine what was going at the other end of the universe but not beyond that drape?

In the middle of the night Bea heard Coreen moaning, "Help me. Lord, help me. I'm freezing."

Bea stood from bed, wobbling, and pushed aside the curtain. Coreen lay with her head thrown back on her pillow, her johnny pulled low as if she had clawed at the neck. Her breasts were exposed, hard and full, rippling with veins; they looked like twin hemispheres carved from mahogany, the North and South Pole rising from each.

"I'm freezing. I'm dying." She was shaking so violently that the bed squeaked beneath her. Her blanket lay on the floor.

Slowly Bea bent and gathered Coreen's blanket. She drew the cotton cloth over her roommate. Her wrist brushed Coreen's arm. Bea flinched away, scorched.

She pulled the cord for the nurse, then tugged the blanket from her own bed and spread it over Coreen, whose shaking didn't stop.

Patrice came. "What's the matter? Tell me what's wrong."

"She's freezing," Bea told her. "She said she feels like she's dying."

Patrice took Bea's arm and led her back. "She's just being melodramatic," Patrice whispered. "The state gives them formula. They can't bear to turn down something for free. I'll get her an ice pack. She'll be fine, don't you worry."

Bea glanced at the curtain. "I'll get a doctor myself."

Patrice stalked from the room. Bea pushed through the drape. She didn't know what to do, so she stood there and waited. Without the window, this side of the room was so gloomy that she almost reached up to switch on the TV.

"Don't."

Her heart jumped.

"Don't let them take him." It seemed to cost Coreen a great deal to speak. "Don't," she repeated.

"I promise," Bea said. But already Coreen had started thrashing again and she didn't seem to hear.

The baby was sleeping facedown in his crib. When Bea lifted him, he hung limp from her hands, surprisingly light compared to her own child. She carried him the way one might carry a puppy, then sat with him on her bed. Was he breathing? He hadn't stirred. She stroked his curls, then his neck. He turned toward her belly, his cheek nestling against her thigh. He moved his lips. Her breasts tingled.

A doctor came. Bea huddled closer to the child, partly for warmth and partly to protect him, from what she didn't know. What would she do if someone tried to take him?

The doctor asked Coreen this or that question; he called her "Miss Jones" and murmured "I see" after each of her answers. Then he slowly explained that she had an infection called en-do-me-tri-tis. "It's really quite rare for a natural birth, but sometimes it happens." He sounded offhand, though Bea knew this was something that women used to die from. "We'll put in an IV—that's an intravenous line—and you'll feel better before long."

The baby in Bea's lap looked up but didn't cry, as if he understood it was in his best interest to lie still. His smooth copper skin reminded Bea of the telescope her father had bought her when she turned twelve. She had held it for hours, until the sun set, certain it would bring her the power to see. The child in her lap seemed to hold this same promise. Unlike her own son, he appeared to want nothing. But how could that be true? How could any child not *want*?

A sweet-faced young woman—Korean? Japanese?—wheeled an IV pole next to Bea's bed. She must have been a medical student, Bea thought; she had the overly serious expression of someone who is hiding how uncertain she feels.

"Here," the student said, "let me take . . . Is that your baby?"

Bea held the boy closer, hiding his face. "You want my roommate, Coreen Jones."

"Oh," the student said. She still seemed confused, but wheeled the pole through the curtain. "Hello," she said. "Don't worry, I'll be done in a minute. It won't hurt one bit."

Bea could hear her roommate mutter, "You ain't got it in."

"Just a minute . . . right there . . ."

"Missed by a mile, girl. Might as well of stuck that thing in my ear." Coreen mumbled these words; if Bea hadn't grown accustomed to hearing Coreen's voice, she wouldn't have known what she had said.

The student kept up her patter—"See, that didn't hurt"—and Coreen stopped complaining. When Bea carried the baby back to his crib his mother lay snoring, the blanket Bea had given her pulled to her chin.

The statistician returned. "I got paid!" She waved a check. "We've got twenty-four hours to create a new me."

Bea was changing Isaac's diaper, holding his ankles in the air with one hand and swabbing yellow stool from his bottom with the other. She hadn't washed her hair since coming to the hospital. She wore tortoiseshell glasses she had picked out in ninth grade. "I'm really very tired."

"Just one little beauty tip?"

Bea stared at the girl. What was the name of that stuff on her eyes? Liner? Mascara? "Maybe you could use less shadow," she said. As she taped Isaac's diaper and wiped his feces from her hands she searched for a phrase from the glamour magazines her mother used to buy. "Let the real you come through."

"The real me?" The girl seemed baffled. "Well, my friends always say I'm a typical redhead."

Bea could hear Coreen groan. "I meant your *best* self," she said. "Let your best self shine through."

"But how?" the girl asked.

Bea shrugged. "That's the same advice I give to all my clients."

The girl nodded gravely. "I'll try it," she said. She again waved the check. "How much do I owe you?"

Bea flapped her hand, a gesture that made her feel both generous and mean.

"Thanks!" the girl said. "I'll let you know how it goes." On her way to the hall she stopped to chat with Coreen. "How *are* you?" she asked. "I just wanted to tell you, I looked in an atlas, and Sierra Leone was right there in West Africa, just like you said!"

Coreen got a visit from a tired-sounding woman who seemed to run the clinic where Coreen had received her prenatal care.

"What's this?" the doctor said. "Who put in this IV?" She summoned Patrice. "Just look at this arm, the way it's all blown up. My patient's IV has been draining into everything *but* her vein — for how long? Ten, fifteen hours? Where do you think all that fluid's been going?"

The doctor couldn't stay — another of her patients was about to deliver — but she gave Patrice instructions as to what to do next.

"I didn't put this in," Patrice grumbled when the doctor had gone. "I would never do a job as sloppy as this."

"Huh," Coreen said. "If I treated hamburger meat as sloppy as you treat the folks in these beds, they would fire my ass."

Coreen was feeling better, but her baby still was sick. "He shits all the time," she told the pediatrician.

"Oh, all newborn babies have frequent movements," he said. He sounded like the same well-meaning young man who had given Isaac his checkup. ("The nurse tells me that you and your baby aren't bonding," he said. "Is there anything I can do?" as shy as a boy whose mother has asked him to unhook her brassiere.)

"Ain't just frequent," Coreen told him. "And the color ain't right." The pediatrician started to say that all newborn babies had odd-colored "movements," but Coreen stopped him. "Don't you think I know what a baby's shit looks like? Didn't I raise myself twins?"

His voice tensed. "I'll look into it. But I'm sure if the nurses had seen anything amiss, I would have been notified."

Bea assumed he was right, until she remembered that, even at her sickest, Coreen had changed her baby's diapers herself.

Coreen's boyfriend came to visit. Bea saw nothing but his running shoes, caked with dry mud, as they moved back and forth beneath the blue curtain. She could hear when he kissed his son, then Coreen.

"Go on," Coreen said. "I'm too sore for that stuff."

The boyfriend, it seemed, drove a moving van or truck. He had been away on a trip to some city out West. How could he have known that Coreen would give birth to their child five weeks early? When no one answered at home he called the hospital from a pay phone, but someone at the switchboard kept cutting him off. He drove without stopping until he reached Boston.

They talked about names. The man suggested Mitchell, after a younger brother who died. But Coreen wasn't sure. "This boy ain't lucky as it is." She spoke softly but didn't mumble. "I can feel it in my bones." Bea heard something in Coreen's voice that she hadn't heard before. Or maybe she was hearing Coreen's voice as it was.

"Never mind your bones," the boyfriend said, laughing. "All you women, nothing you like better than worrying. Hell, we got us a son. Come to Daddy, little Mitchell. First thing's gonna happen now your daddy's come back, he's gonna buy you some pants!"

Coreen's fever returned, no one knew why. The doctors spoke to her kindly, but they said she couldn't leave. She told them that her twins were only three years old. She might lose her job, she said. Precisely, they said, what she needed was rest, which she wouldn't get at home.

In the middle of the night, though she must have felt ill, Coreen changed her baby's diaper for the third or fourth time. Then she rang for the nurse.

"Look at these diapers! You tell me his shit's supposed to be red."

"Oh!" Patrice said. Bea heard the nurse's shoes slap the linoleum as she ran down the hall. She returned with a doctor whose voice Bea didn't recognize. He had a rich, soothing accent—English, or Australian. He paused between phrases as if to gauge the responses of someone whose reactions might be different from his.

He was . . . concerned, he told Coreen, that her son might have . . . a serious form of diarrhea. An infection in the bowel. Not so rare, really, especially for babies like hers, who had been born premature. They were taking him to Children's Hospital, just down the street. She could see him as soon as she was feeling "more perky." In the meantime, he said, they would send word how he was.

An orderly wheeled the child out the door. Bea thought of pushing through the curtain to comfort Coreen, but what could she say? That the doctors at Children's were the best in the world? That she hadn't broken her promise not to let them take him?

Early the next morning Bea dressed herself, then her son. Bundled in the snowsuit Bea's mother had sent, Isaac seemed thoughtful, as if contemplating this latest change in his life. She took a deep breath and pushed aside the curtain, holding the gift her colleagues had sent; she had eaten one pear, but the rest of the pyramid of fruit was intact. She waited for her roommate to say *Keep your damn apples*. But Coreen didn't remove her gaze from the woman in sequins spinning a shiny wheel on TV.

Bea set the fruit on the night stand. "I hope you feel better soon. I hope your baby is all right." She tried not to wish that her roommate would thank her. "Is there anything I can do?"

Coreen turned to face her. For some reason, Bea thought that her roommate would tell her to pray. But Coreen shook her head no and turned back to the spinning wheel on TV.

From the moment Bea came home she had no trouble nursing. She locked the doors and pulled down the shades. She peeled off Isaac's diaper, T-shirt, and hat and gave him a bath. Seeing him naked and whole the first time, she felt a catch in her throat, a pressure in her chest. She assumed this was love, but the word seemed too weak, as if she had grown up calling pink "red," and then, in her thirties, seen crimson or scarlet.

Isaac slept by her side. Whenever he was hungry she gave him a breast. Milk spurted in his mouth so quickly it choked him; she needed to pump out the excess, which sprayed from each nipple like water from a shower head. He would suck half an hour at each breast, if she let him. How could she watch his face for so long and still not be bored? Her elation, she knew, was hormonal. But who would have thought that a chemical substance could produce this effect? If vials of oxytocin could be bought at a store, who would drink alcohol or use drugs? She hadn't suspected that of all the emotions a human being could feel, this . . . tenderness . . . would be the one she craved most.

135

When she felt a bit stronger, Bea telephoned the hospital and asked a nurse in obstetrics if Coreen Jones had gone home. Yes she had, the nurse said. And her baby? Bea asked. "Just a moment," the nurse said. A few minutes later she got back on the line and said that the baby had been transferred to Children's, that was all the information she could release.

When Bea called Children's Hospital, she introduced herself as Dr. Beatrice Weller, which, technically, she was, and learned that a patient listed only as "male infant Jones" had died two days earlier. She said, "Yes," and hung up.

That afternoon, she borrowed a pouch from the family next door, strapped Isaac inside and walked to the T. As she stood by the turnstile, struggling to get some change from her pocket, someone behind her said, "Honey, don't rush. What a mother really needs isn't a pouch, it's an extra pair of hands."

The woman who'd said this was at least six feet tall, with soft, sculpted hair and perfect brown skin. She wore a yellow cashmere suit and enormous brass earrings. Bea wondered if she might be one of the anchors on the local evening news, then decided that such a celebrity wouldn't be taking the T.

The woman dropped a token in the box for Bea's fare. Bea tried to repay her. But the woman lifted one palm, pushed through the gate and, briefcase to chest, ran to catch her train.

When Bea got to the hospital she went straight to Room 3. She said that she had come to buy a picture for a friend who was ill, wrote a check for twenty dollars and was handed a portrait in a flimsy pink folder with bears along one edge. Clipped to the front was the form each mother had filled out: MOTHER'S NAME . . . ADDRESS . . . Coreen's writing was shaky; Bea remembered her leaning on the woman in front.

She opened the folder. Yellow pinafore. Curls. Full lips. She thought of mailing the portrait, but decided to follow through with her plan. To hand a person an envelope and offer your condolences for the death of her child seemed a minimum requirement for living on Earth.

She took the subway to a neighborhood she had never been to before. The three-decker houses weren't all that much different from the ones where Bea lived, but the smallest details—a pair of red sneakers dangling from a telephone wire, an unopened pack of gum lying in a gutter—seemed enlarged and mysterious. Most of the houses here were enclosed by steel fences. German shepherds and Dobermans strained at their leashes and barked as Bea passed. As he slept, Isaac stirred; with her cheek to his soft spot she could feel his brain pulse.

She finally found the right address. Three rusty mailboxes hung askew on the porch, an eagle on each: HERRERO, GREEN, JONES. Had Bea really believed that she could ring Coreen's doorbell and explain why she had come? When Coreen saw the photo of her dead son, she would scream. Maybe she would faint. Besides this, Bea was holding a healthy baby in her pouch, and that, more than anything—her job, or her race, what she did or didn't say—would make Coreen hate her.

A light flickered on behind a third-story window. Bea pictured Coreen lying on her bed, stone mute with grief. Her boyfriend came in. *Don't worry, sweetheart, we'll have another baby. It wasn't your fault.* Bea wondered where the twins were. And Lena? Coreen's mother? What about Coreen's job? Would they allow her time off? How useless the eye, she thought, without the imagination to inform it, to make sense of the darkness surrounding the light.

A child started crying in the building next door. Bea's breasts began to tingle; in his pouch, Isaac stirred. She slid the folder in the mailbox. Milk flowed from her nipples, soaking her blouse. She hurried to the T station, where she zippered her parka so that only Isaac's head poked from the top.

Her last night in the hospital, Bea had lain with her hands pressed against her ears as Coreen changed her baby's diaper again and again. By then, Bea herself had come down with a fever. Every joint ached. Her breasts had swollen grossly. They were lumpy, rock hard, as if someone had pumped them full of concrete. Another few drops of milk and they would burst.

And yet they kept filling. Every time Coreen's baby whimpered, milk surged into Bea's breasts, pushing through ducts that felt tiny and clogged, like irrigation ditches silted with clay. In another few moments, she would be forced to get up and stagger down the hall and try to stop Patrice from feeding Isaac the formula she had warned Bea she would give him. Bea longed to feel his mouth sucking her nipples, sucking and sucking, easing her pain. In the meantime, she lay there, palms against her ears, her breasts filling with milk for another woman's child.

For Fathers of Girls

STEPHEN DUNN

for Susanne

When sperm leaves us
and we cockadoodledo
and our wives rise like morning

the children we start
are insignificant as bullets
that get lodged, say,

in a field somewhere
in the midwest.
If we are thinking then

it is probably of sleep
or the potency of rest, or
the one-hand catch we made

long ago at the peak of our lives.
Later, though, in a dream
we may imagine something in the womb

of our heads, neither boy nor girl,
nothing quite so simple.
But when we wake, our wives are

breathing like the wounded
on the whitest street in the world.
We are there

we are wearing conspicuous masks
for the first time,
our eyes show the sweat

from our palms.
Suddenly we are fathers
of girls: purply, covered with slime

we could kiss. There's a cry,
and the burden of living up
to ourselves is upon us again.

The Welcoming

Coming Home from the Hospital after My Son's Birth

JIM DANIELS

The chimney next door tilts
precarious, just
like it did yesterday.

In the street, a red sports-
car revs and stalls,
good for a laugh.

I wipe my tears.
I strum a very tiny
air guitar.

The Welcoming

EDWARD HIRSCH

After the long drought
                and the barren silence,
After seven years of fertility doctors
And medicine men in clinics
                    dreaming of rain,
After the rainfall and the drugs
                      that never engendered a child—

What is for others nature
                is for us culture:
Social workers and lawyers,
                    home studies and courtrooms,
Passports, interlocutory orders, a birth certificate
         that won't be delivered for a year,
                  a haze of injunctions, jurisdictions, handshakes,
Everyone standing around in dark suits
                  saying yes, we think so, yes . . .

It has been less than a month and already
I want to bring you
                out of the darkness,
             out of the deep pockets of silence . . .
While you were spending your fifth day
                    under bright lights in a new world,
We were traveling
              from Rome to New Orleans,
Twenty-three hours of anguish and airplanes,
Instructions in two languages,
                music from cream-colored headsets,

jet lag instead of labor,
And on the other end a rainbow
                              of streamers in the French Quarter,
            a row of fraternity boys celebrating
                  in Jackson Square, the trolleys
                  buzzing up and down St. Charles Avenue,
The stately run-down southern mansions
Winking
            behind the pecan trees and the dark-leaved magnolias.

You were out there somewhere,
                  blinking, feeding omnivorously
                        from a nurse's arms, sleeping,
But who could sleep anymore
                  beside the innocent and the oblivious,
      who could dream?

How unreal it was to drive
                        through the narrow, twisted streets
            of an unfamiliar American city
            and then arrive at the empty bungalow
                        of a friend of a friend.
Outside, the trees waved slightly
                        under a cradle of moonlight
While, inside, the floorboards sagged
            and creaked, the air conditioner kicked on
                        in the next room, in autumn,
      an invisible cat cried — a baby's cry —
      and roamed through the basement at 4 A.M.

All night long we were moored
            to the shoreline of the bay windows,
                  to the edge of a bent sky
            where the moon rocked

and the stars were tiny crescent fish
        swimming through amniotic fluids.
There was a deep rumbling underground,
And our feelings came in and went out, like waves.

By the vague tremors of dawn,
By the first faint pinkish-blue light
        of morning rising in the east,
All we could think about
        was the signing of papers
            in a neighboring parish,
     the black phone that was going to shout
        at any moment, just once,
  our lawyer's slow drive to the hospital
      with an infant seat
    strapped into her car. You were waiting:
Little swimmer, the nurses at Touro
     didn't want to relinquish you
        to the afterlife of our arms . . .

But so it was written:

On the sixth day,
After five days and nights on this earth,
You were finally delivered
        into our keeping,
A wrinkled traveler from a faraway place
      who had journeyed a great distance,
A sweet aboriginal angel
      with your own life,
A throbbing bundle of instincts and nerves —
    perfect fingers, perfect toes,
      shiny skin, blue soulful eyes
        deeply set in your perfectly shaped head —

Oh wailing messenger,
Oh baleful full-bodied crier
                    of the abandoned and the chosen,
Oh trumpet of laughter, oh Gabriel,
                              joy everlasting . . .

Shrinking the Uterus

CATHY SONG

After the birth of my son, my mother moves in.
She enlists the help of her sisters, my aunts,
who appear in full force
with chicken broth drenched in whiskey
to tide me over, a preliminary
dish to the masterpiece
they spend days in my kitchen
preparing — ju gerk, pig's feet soup,
which I can hear rattling on the stove top
as if the pig's feet were tap dancing
to a simmering frenzy.

The stew is sickeningly sweet,
vinegar and brown sugar
boiled down to a thick caramel tar.
I am ordered to eat it —
or else in my old age
I'll have "plenny pilikia" — woman's trouble.
Pig's feet help shrink the uterus,
which after birth is a flabby bag of muscle.
Pig's feet help get rid of the old blood.
So I am told.

I am told a lot of things.
My mother scares me with a string of wives' tales,
and my aunts concur.
I must keep off my feet.
I must keep them warm.
I must keep away from windows.
I mustn't, under any circumstances,
wash my hair for a month.
Ancient Chinese birth control,
my father says with a wink.
My mother gives him the what-does-he-know look.
And already, tsk, tsk, I am spoiling the baby.

The wind is howling
when commandeered by my mother
I shuffle in my house slippers toward the kitchen,
my hair matted with the sweat of labor,
my mind rice gruel from lack of sleep.
Who would find me
desirable in this hour of my life?
She leads me to the table,
offers me at last the triumphant gelatinous hooves —
silent pearly knobs of cartilage
bobbing like dentures in a porcelain bowl.

Her First Week

SHARON OLDS

She was so small I would scan the crib a half-second
to find her, face-down in a corner, limp
as something gently flung down, or fallen
from some sky an inch above the mattress. I would
tuck her arm along her side
and slowly turn her over. She would tumble
over part by part, like a load
of damp laundry, in the dryer, I'd slip
a hand in, under her neck,
slide the other under her back,
and evenly lift her up. Her little bottom
sat in my palm, her chest contained
the puckered, moire sacs, and her neck—
I was afraid of her neck, once I almost
thought I heard it quietly snap,
I looked at her and she swivelled her slate
eyes and looked at me. It was in
my care, the creature of her spine, like the first
chordate, as if the history
of the vertebrate had been placed in my hands.
Every time I checked, she was still
with us—someday, there would be a human
race. I could not see it in her eyes,
but when I fed her, gathered her
like a loose bouquet to my side and offered
the breast, greyish-white, and struck with
minuscule scars like creeks in sunlight, I
felt she was serious, I believed she was willing to stay.

Babylove

CORINNE DEMAS

They are the only people awake in their part of the world now, creatures on the wrong shift. Even the barred owls — there are three of them posted around the house — have ceased their calls: four interrogatives, and a descending mournful cry. This is the time when the animals who are too timid for daylight and the animals who hunt them have the earth to themselves. Shrews and mice and rabbits and foxes and strange worms that may not even have names. The earth, not large enough to accommodate all creatures at once, has devised this plan: some sleep while others live. Each territory has two distinct populations, whose lives are secret from each other.

The baby, who sleeps in a bassinet next to the mother's side of the bed, has been crying for several seconds now. In the mother's ordinary life, seconds are periods of time so insignificant they are rarely tallied, but in this new phase of her life seconds have taken on significance. Each second that the baby cries is long enough for her to have dissertations of thought. Now she debates the question "will he go back to sleep?" But her body, which, since the baby's birth, has a direct linkage to her heart, responds on its own. She sits up in bed, and her arms reach out towards the bassinet.

The baby in the bassinet, like many of the offspring of his parents' acquaintances, has been given a three-syllable name from the Old Testament. His parents have every intention to call him by it. Theirs is not a generation that takes well to nicknames. Yet the baby's name, at the moment, is theoretical only. He is The Baby, and their own names in turn, have flickered off somewhere. They are now Mommy and Daddy, and even when they speak to the baby they refer to themselves in the third person, as if they want to spare their baby, for the moment, confusion over the shared nature of the pronoun "I."

The mother thinks the baby is the most beautiful creature in the world, but in fact, as babies go, he is one of the homelier ones. He may grow up to be a man women find attractive, but now his features are indistinct behind a layer of fat, and his eyes, which are open only rarely, have a swimmy colorless quality. A red birthmark perches at the edge of one brow. It is not really disfiguring, more something that you instinctively want to brush away. The mother, who in her pregnant months tortured herself with all the possibilities of deformities known to man, is relieved by this tiny imperfection. This small blemish marks her son as human and will protect him from harm. No gods will be tempted to tamper with his perfection.

The mother hunches over the bassinet and is about to gather the baby up in her arms, but just at that second he pauses in his crying and lets out a little noise which is closer to a sigh. The father, who had begun to waken with the baby's cries and the mother's movements, seizes this reprieve and shifts back into sleep. The mother hovers, ready, by the bassinet, until she is certain the crying has really ceased, and then she climbs back into bed and settles upright, against the pillows. She is still awaiting the baby's next move. She watches the digital clock on the bureau across the room. The seconds move more quickly now, as if making up for their previous languor. The numerals are not mere bands of light, but are actual numbers on little squares that get dropped into place. She thinks of them as a miniature billboard displayed by Lilliputians — who are now working frantically to catch up.

Beside her, in bed, the father clears his throat in his sleep, as if he is about to speak, but whatever speech he has been making in his dreams he keeps to himself. The mother, who used to be an expansive dreamer, no longer dreams. She has not slept more than three hours straight since the baby was born, and when she sleeps she has no energy to waste on dreams. She turns now to watch her husband, wonders about his dreams. The baby is their first child, and both mother and father are old enough so that they thought they might never have one. She is forty, her husband is forty-two. They had been married a number of years before they began to think they were ready for parenthood, and they discovered that it was a feat not so easily accomplished. In fact, when the baby was finally conceived it was after they each had given up hope — though they did not speak of this to each other until afterwards. The mother sees her long trial as a just punishment for what she thinks of as her ignorant selfishness for so many years. She had been afraid for her career, afraid for her marriage. She had thought of a baby as a rival for herself. Now her mistake is obvious. She had thought a baby would be Other, and the baby is, unquestionably, irrevocably, Self. Though she doesn't believe in God, she believes in some sort of divine interference. The sense of wonder that they are parents flickers in and out during her conscious hours and sustains her through all the weariness she feels. She sees herself and her husband as part of the elect.

It is quiet now in the bedroom. The baby is sleeping soundlessly; the outside world goes about its business in silence. The mother turns to watch the father's sleeping face. She is so accustomed to the baby's smallness that the father's head seems enormous, his features seem like curiosities. She has to look at his face for a long time before it recedes to its familiar proportion again.

In the evenings, before the baby was born, the father worked on a Noah's ark for him. He had started with the ark itself and then had begun making the pairs of animals, cutting them out with a jigsaw and sanding them so smooth that the pine felt like butter. He had made alligators, hippos, kangaroos, camels, and sheep and was up to the geese when the baby was born. The mother had loved the smell of the wood he worked, and she had loved watching him, his large hands forming the small figures. Now, that memory of him holds her, and as if to make it more real she reaches out and lays her palm on her husband's bare shoulder. Her palm remembers — remembers flesh, remembers something more.

She runs her fingers along her husband's shoulder, then across his chest: skin, hair, sweat — braille in the night. She nuzzles down against her husband's shoulder. She licks a small circle and then sinks her mouth down, cups his flesh in her lips. She would not actually awaken him, but she wants him to waken. For the first time since the baby was born she forgets for a minute that she is a mother. She presses herself against her husband's side. He is still asleep, but his free arm moves up, and he reaches for her across his chest. She takes his hand and lays it on her breast.

"Touch me," she asks him softly. "Please touch me."

His hand rests for a minute on her body, but then he moves his shoulder and his hand drops down against his hip. He coughs once and his mouth stays half-open, his lips moving slightly with his breath.

The mother leans back against the pillows. Her breasts have filled up, and they are so hard they feel like wood. She gets up slowly and leans over the bassinet. The baby is sleeping still. She touches the side of his cheek. Milk starts streaming down from both breasts. She scoops the sleeping baby up in her arms and gets back into bed. She braces her elbow against her husband's side and lifts the baby up in place. Even in his sleep he turns his face toward her breast. She pushes her nipple into the baby's parted mouth.

"Suck, darling," she whispers. "Suck. Suck."

The Man Who Would Be a Mother

HERBERT SCOTT

The stirrings in his chest
are maternal, mild. He imagines
giving suck, the gentle ooze,
the child's lips still forming
around his nipple. He wipes away
the last drop with his thumb,
lifts it to his tongue. Milk.
The first taste in his mouth again.

He would say to his children:
You were once in my belly. This
is how you fed before you were born.
This is where I held you,
child on a rope of blood.
This is my mark on your belly.
When you came into your life,
they held you up for me to see,
as if I were dangling from you, your child.

If I am not your mother,
and you do not rise from my body,
it is not because I would not have it.
Take my hands, as if they were
your face, and when I am dead,
and this flesh unlocks the bones,
imagine birth from my body,
a garden of children blooming.

from *The Velveteen Father*

JESSE GREEN

Three

One week after he first heard the little boy described, Andy was on a plane to pick him up. He could still back out, if necessary, for any reason or no reason at all: *He's too sick. He's too little. He looks like a monkey.* People had changed their minds for less. It was really a matter of imagination. Some birth parents instantaneously loved the little blob handed over to them: They saw it come from the mother's own body, and could find their own features in its shrieking face. Adopting parents had to take a leap of faith. They had to believe that the child handed over all neat in his swaddling would some day grow to look like them, or feel like them at least.

Andy arrived, late that night, at the cheap motel the foster mother had suggested. He brought with him little more than a book and a comb and a diaper bag waiting to be filled. He called me to see how Erez was doing (he was asleep) and to say good night. Then there was a knock at his door. "Is everything all right?" the desk clerk asked. "Do you have enough blankets?" He lingered, smiling and sheepish.

"Thank you, yes," said Andy, closing him out politely.

It would not have been apparent to the desk clerk that Andy was here to pick up a son and that he had another one back home, not to mention a spouse. He would have seen a handsome man with a New York accent and almost no luggage. He would have seen availability, whereas what Andy saw in himself was satiety. Fear and exhaustion, of course, but mostly a sense of impending completion. The construction of his life was almost topped off (as builders of skyscrapers like to say): A flag could be planted on the uppermost beam, and the rest of the work would be details.

Nevertheless, ringing the bell at the foster mother's shiny house in a wooded suburban development the next morning, he was almost sick with nervousness; perhaps the breakfast of *huevos rancheros* at a Mexican diner hadn't helped matters. But Pat turned out to be a cool blonde in her late thirties with a calmingly matter-of-fact attitude, as if Andy had answered an ad for a grandfather clock she was hoping to sell, and had come to inspect it. Foster parenting was her business if not her passion; taking in a newborn from time to time, at fifty-five dollars a day plus expenses, allowed her to stay at home with her own brood of four, the youngest an adopted "special needs" child who was even now creeping around on the floor, watching the interesting transaction.

Pat went into her sales pitch, though it wasn't anything so crude; her interest in closing the deal was largely unselfish. It would have been to her financial advantage to hold on to her visiting babies longer, but emotionally she must have learned not to get too attached. She knew it was best for everyone involved if the baby was placed as soon as possible, so she did what she could to make that happen. "He sleeps well, eats heartily, and is sweet as can be," she told Andy while leading him to the bassinet. "One of my kids even said, 'Oh, this one's cute, we ought to keep him,'" which led Andy to expect another Erez.

We all learn to expect the wrong thing. The three-week-old baby was asleep in the bassinet; how many other babies had slept there? This one had a bright-red scrunched-up face and a stripe of black hair across his skull like a Mohawk. When he opened his eyes a few minutes later they were almond, feline, tiny slits in a pie. He weighed nothing, of course, and yet he was solid, and then he let out an enormous cry. He was healthy, all right. Andy fed him a demi-bottle of formula that Pat had prepared, then changed his diaper, the size of a thank-you note. He did all this somewhat mechanically, worried he was not bonding quickly enough (though less than twenty minutes had passed) and looking constantly into the baby's face for a sign that this was his son.

"He's all red and scrunchy," he whispered on the phone. "I know I'm not supposed to care, but Erez was so cute."

"Erez was a Caesarean, right? They're always cute," I answered. "And this one was two weeks premature, so it's really like he's just a week old, and lots of babies look squashed at that age."

"I suppose . . ."

But why was I arguing on the side of the baby — if it *was* the side of the baby? I had not seen him, could barely picture him; even if I had and could, on what basis would I form an opinion? Yet I had an opinion. This is the child fate offered; let us acquiesce, as a shtetl bride acquiesces to a marriage arranged by her father. In an age of individuality and romance, of children virtually by design, this was, of course, a throwback, a submission. But for once in my life I felt submissive. Let us take him, I said, and wait for the love to come later.

Four

It would not take long. By the time they landed at Newark Airport that night, Andy and the boy were father and son. Not yet officially: Though he had signed temporary custody papers ("I agree to take this child into my home in the same manner as if the child had been born to me . . ."), Andy would not be his legal father until the adoption was "finalized," before a state judge, six months to a year down the road. But the emotional bond had begun to set the minute Andy left Pat's house — a bond not like a manacle but like glue. It had taken time for the two halves to marry, but not much time. Now they were one; even the stewardesses said so.

I arrived at the airport early, having hired a car service on the assumption that Andy would be too tired (and I too nervous) to drive. I was right about myself at least: I waited for fifteen minutes by the carousels, my heart jumping at every baby's squeal, but forgetting that Andy had checked no luggage. When I finally realized my mistake I raced in a panic around the terminal. Finally I spotted them in the glassy emptiness of the departures instead of the arrivals concourse: Andy in a leather jacket bulging with bottles, the baby in a tiny car seat that TWA had helpfully labeled "Special Handling."

I could hardly see the little boy, all but mummified in the puffy down sack in which Andy had dressed him. He was, remarkably, asleep. I pushed aside a piece of the hood in order to get a closer view; he looked a bit like an angry monkey, but it didn't matter. I kissed him on his hot plum cheek, and so I kissed his father.

"He's here," he said. We stood crying in the vast concourse.

After a few minutes we transferred the baby and ourselves into the hired car. The driver tried to help, but there was little we would let him do. He did take extra care to avoid sharp turns and sudden stops as we headed toward the Verrazano, and smiled at us, or raised an eyebrow, in the rearview mirror. Did he want to speak? In any case, I did not want to hear him; on the ride to the airport we'd already had a disturbing conversation. He'd seemed eager to be friendly. Perhaps, having picked me up at my apartment in the Village, he made some quick assumptions, just as the motel desk clerk made some quick assumptions about Andy. "You are meeting a friend?" he asked; from his accent he seemed to be an Arab.

"Yes," I said, instantly flummoxed. "My friend is just returning with the new baby . . . that is being adopted." I had not tried to use this kind of passive, genderless construction in years, and was rusty at it. What did I think it would accomplish, anyway? He'd see Andy soon enough. But I'd rather him see than have me explain, so I said what I said with a tone of finality in hopes it would derail the discussion.

"Your girlfriend?" he asked, doubtfully.

"No. A guy." I felt myself blush.

We were stuck in line for the Holland Tunnel, moving only ten feet a minute; at this rate the conversation seemed likely to continue until I actually died.

"And you do that guy-guy thing?" asked the driver.

Though the wording was creepy, he did not seem hostile. His English was good but not good enough to make clear the nature of his curiosity. Was he personally interested in the guy-guy thing? Just making chitchat?

Before I could answer—and I have no idea what I would have said—he added, sadly, or so I thought, "In my country, you know what they do to you?"

I wasn't sure whether he meant me personally, or people like me, or even people like him. In any case, I warily shook my head no.

He made a gesture with his right hand, removing it from the steering wheel and slashing six inches of air. "See?"

"I think so."

Now he drove in silence as I grilled Andy about the trip just completed: What did you sign? What did people say? Between us, the boy in his car seat was all but inanimate: an expensive shopping bag. Ahead of us, the driver's eyebrow popping up in the mirror from time to time reminded me that the happiness Andy and I felt in each other, let alone in this sleeping monkey-baby, was a happiness much of the world would punish severely. It made me feel that the little boy wasn't the only delicate package being transferred to safety. We, too, were adoptees, remanded into our own adult care, charged with creating, over and over, better worlds to live in.

Erez and the baby-sitter were both asleep when we got back to Andy's, but Chauncey wasn't. He came over and sniffed the boy, whom we had laid on a receiving blanket for his consideration. He seemed to find the new person acceptable; at any rate, he went back to his favorite spot and curled up. After putting the boy in the bassinet and winding up the musical clown, so did we. For one hour.

Five

"May the one who comes be blessed": Thus began the circumcision service two days later. Sixty people crowded into Andy's apartment for the noon affair, including dozens of delegates from Andy's rangy family and three from mine: my mother, father, and nephew. All were kind enough, upon arriving, not to mention that we looked wooden and sallow, with raccoon rings around our eyes; we had barely slept since the boy arrived forty hours before, and our hearts (I could feel Andy's, too) were clanking, loud and irregular, like the radiators.

At least the baby was getting cuter; what sleep we had lost, he had found and kept. His capuchin face had begun to unfold, his redness to recede. Everyone admired his sequin eyes: Is he Chinese? they asked.

"No, Jewish," I inevitably said. "As you will see."

Not *all* would see. We hired a sitter to keep Erez and my nephew busy in the nursery during the circumcision itself; if we had made our peace with the implications of the surgery on the baby, we were not so sure of its effect on a toddler who might catch a glimpse. Probably we should have hired a sitter for the adult men, too. They visibly blanched as the mohelet set out her arcane equipment, which looked both surgical and culinary. The adult women, more familiar with blood and cooking, were matter-of-fact and stalwart.

This was the same mohelet—a handsome woman in a nubbly pink suit—who had circumcised Erez twenty-two months earlier. With the air of some-one used to explaining herself, she politely brushed aside nervous queries about her authority: "Did you know," she countered, "that females performed the rite in ancient Israel?" As a woman and a convert to Judaism (not to men-tion a plastic surgeon) she had clearer ideas about her role than did run-of-the-mill mohels, most of whom had inherited their ancient sideline unthinkingly, as others inherit a dental practice. Few would even perform a bris on a child born of Catholic parents, let alone a child adopted by a gay man to be raised with his boyfriend. But this one did so happily, recognizing perforce an idea of Judaism that is more inclusive than the one formulated by medieval rabbis. Indeed, in her mimeographed script for the service, she had slightly doctored the traditional prayers so as to include among the litany of patriarchs the names of suppressed matriarchs as well. Perhaps this was only fitting, since the mother had been suppressed in our story, too. Still, in the manner of all things defensive and politically correct, it was as awkward as it was moving: Sarah, Rebekah, Leah, and Rachel had been pieced into the Hebrew text by hand, unevenly, like a ransom note.

There was nothing politically correct about what followed. Onto her fore-head, the mohelet strapped a lamp, which glowed and shimmered like a halo-gen diadem. Then she withdrew from her satchel a large flat board fitted with Velcro restraints. Calmly she instructed me how to hold the baby utterly still upon the board, lest his legs close and ruin the job. In the event, this took all my strength, for he struggled mightily—not, it seemed, from any pain, but from the insult of being butterflied. After saying a prayer, the mohelet dipped the edge of a napkin into a glass of sweet red wine, twisted it into the shape of a nipple and offered it as a mild anesthetic—to the baby, that is, though I could have used it. While he sucked hungrily, she leaned forward and com-pleted the cutting, at which point the baby pooped and promptly fell asleep.

"Our God and God of our mothers and fathers," the mohelet chanted, having added the mothers, "sustain this child and let him be known in the house of Israel as . . ."

Here the script offered only a blank, as life did, too. Andy had wanted to name the child Juan, a nod to Janet and to the boy's Mexican origins. Zev and Wolf, rejected for Erez, poked up their feral heads again, only to be heartlessly quashed. "You're overcompensating," I told Andy. I suggested honoring his mother with her maiden name—Emanuel—instead; if this were the boy's middle name it would leave us free to choose something pretty and preferably nonanimal for the first. Andy agreed, in part because he liked my suggestion—Lucas, for light—and in part because he thought it sounded ever so slightly like a name that might still mean "wolf."

". . . let him be known in the house of Israel as Lucas Emanuel," the mohelet continued. "May he bring much joy to his parents in the months and years to come."

With that and a few more prayers, Lucas was a proper Jew, if not to the Orthodox at least to us. But what did that mean: a proper Jew? I was too weak to consider—and oddly famished. I knelt beside my mother's chair and burst out crying. She patted my head, as she always had; my father offered to get me some food from the deli spread Andy had ordered.

"Where do you think it went?" asked my mother a moment later. "You know: *it*. I saw her put it in a napkin, then suddenly it was gone."

"Oh my God," I said, scanning the room for Chauncey.

Apnea

HUNT HAWKINS

My infant son, Samuel, sleeps in his crib,
hunched forward like a small Mohammedan,
while I watch in the dark room,
unable to sleep, listening to his breathing.
The doctors say we all stop many times
each night, but decide to start again.
Two miles away the trucks on the interstate
sizzle. I realize how hard it is
not to think of myself as watched,
if only by some small man inside my head
who keeps everything going. Does he have
a little cot in there, does he ever sleep?
Outside a confused mockingbird starts to sing
long before dawn. The furnace goes on and off,
keeping the house warm. A bit later
the refrigerator does the same, a countermove.
Samuel's chest keeps heaving. Maybe
the world just happens, but sometimes it doesn't.
I can see I will spend the rest of my life
hoping my son will want to breathe.

Gas

BELLE WARING

The adults are getting desperate.
Your mother the Proustian scholar
is too exhausted to spell *souvenir*.
Dad's face has turned into a twitch.

Please, what are you trying to tell us?
What good does it do to scream all night?
You little red yowl, would you forgive us
if we three, your mother and father and me

piled into the car, blasted the radio
loud as it goes, barreled out of town
without you? Here's my trump card: swaddle
you tight as a basketball, strap you into your

windup swing, set you rocking like a metronome.
You gape at the light the way an old geezer
stares at his hands. Maybe your last life in Newark,
New Jersey, retired you to a greasy armchair

where you slouched down, smoked
cheroots, and cursed God. Is there
something you'd like to forget?

Changing Diapers

GARY SNYDER

How intelligent he looks!
   on his back
   both feet caught in my one hand
   his glance set sideways,
   on a giant poster of Geronimo
   with a Sharp's repeating rifle by his knee.

I open, wipe, he doesn't even notice
   nor do I.
Baby legs and knees
   toes like little peas
   little wrinkles, good-to-eat,
   eyes bright, shiny ears,
   chest swelling drawing air,

No trouble, friend,
   you and me and Geronimo
   are men.

Babyshit Serenade

ALICIA OSTRIKER

Nothing is ever the same, when you've put in time cleaning babyshit.
Some hypothetical quality goes out of life —
Something theoretical, something noble.
Right on . . . I mean there it is,
What they call a "dirty" diaper but it's really a shitty diaper,
Wet ones are elegant, relatively, and there you are,
Paying necessary attention to the perpetually unique,
Perpetually fresh consistency, happy if it's a coherent lump
In itself, unhappy if mushy and clinging to that delicious
Otherwise charming bottom . . . in the rhythm of the thing.

    After such knowledge, what forgiveness? Think
    The fantasy life of males sustains itself on not changing shitty diapers,
    The fantasy life of women, on pretending not to, but ah,
    Self-delusion is not so easy
    In the wake of infant fece
                    The hand that rocks the cradle wipes the poop
    So that even if Prince Daffodil did come riding up on a foaming charger
    To carry us away from all this
    To a life of poetic sensitivity
    He would have to kiss our hand, and we would know,
    Even if we didn't inform him.

Sleep

GARY KRIST

Donald's eyes were closing just as the London markets opened.

Paul Brockman, standing over his infant son's crib in Piedmont, New York — three thousand miles from the opening bell in London — glanced at his watch. It was 3:32 A.M., and Donald, thank God, was finally showing the signs of imminent sleep: the licking of thick lips, the enormous, oddly petulant sigh, the lolling of veiny head from side to side. He'd be gone in thirty seconds, Paul guessed. A minute tops. Paul leaned over in the faint blue radiance of the Popeye night-light and put his hand on his son's hot, damp hair. Sleep well, he said silently, enviously.

That was when the telephone rang in the living room.

"Christ," Paul hissed aloud. He looked down anxiously at his son's face, but Donald was already sleeping ferociously — mouth gaping, forehead wrinkled with determination, at the stage when nothing short of artillery or the sound of his mother's voice could rouse him.

Paul made a last adjustment of the blanket and then stepped out to the living room to answer the phone. He knew that the call had to be London. The Tokyo market had already closed, and everyone in the New York office was still asleep — as Paul himself should have been, with Harriet, his wife, snoring away in the luxurious depths of their chestnut sleigh bed down the hall. Last night had been Harriet's turn to sit up with Donald. The two of them alternated odd and even dates; it was an agreement they had worked out together, a system. The only flaw in the system, Paul thought, was that Harriet, on leave from her job at Price Waterhouse, couldn't sit up with Tokyo and London on the nights when Paul was supposed to be sleeping.

"Disasterville, Paul. We've got trouble." It was Derek Peabody, the deputy rep of Paul's firm in London. Paul had never met Derek Peabody, but he knew his voice well enough. It was high-pitched, overly jocular, and — at least at 3:35 A.M. — deeply annoying.

"Okay, give it to me," Paul said, collapsing into the couch and pressing his hot eyelids.

"Renzer is down three and an eighth at the opening and sinking fast. So's the rest of the market, but not as badly."

"So our deal . . ."

"Obsolete would be my guess. Hey, I just work here."

"Does Tokyo know yet?" Paul asked.

"I leave it in your capable hands, guy. I've got phones beeping off the hook here. Bye now."

Paul hung up the phone. He stood a moment, watching the tendons move beneath the smooth skin of his telephone hand. A three-plus-point drop was bad, he knew — so bad that everyone involved would have to know as soon as possible. That was Paul's responsibility. He was the coordinator on this deal, the "harmonizer," as his boss, Pete, liked to say. In his more cynical moments, Paul would define "harmonizer" as the person who wasn't allowed to sing but who took the rap for any sour notes. And it had certainly been easier to harmonize deals in the days before 2 A.M. feedings and the various other gurps and gurgles that would rouse him from bed every other night.

Paul stopped himself. He thought of that helpless, all-powerful presence in the crib down the hall. "Priorities," he told himself firmly.

The first number he punched into the phone was Ben Farley's in Tokyo. As it rang, Paul looked again at his watch: late afternoon, early evening in Tokyo. Ben was probably in transit. "Hello, Kimiko," he said when Ben's wife picked up the phone. "It's Paul from the New York office. How are you?"

"Very good, Paul, thank you." He had never met Kimiko Farley, just as he had never met Derek Peabody, or Roger Billings's daughter in Hong Kong. They were all just voices to him, currents on a telephone wire with personalities attached.

"Well, we're not so good on this side, businesswise. Ben around?"

"Sorry, Paul. Not home from work yet."

"I figured as much."

"His cell phone is still out. But I have him call you the second he comes in."

"Ask him to keep trying if it's busy. It probably will be."

Pete Demiehl in New York, the next person on Paul's list, was somewhat less gracious. "This better be a calamity, at four in the morning, Brockman," he said, only half kidding. Paul explained to him quietly that it *was* a calamity. Renzer was their biggest pending deal. "Set up an early meeting," Pete growled, his voice still heavy with sleep. "E-mail the details so everybody's up to speed by then."

"How early is early?"

Pete paused a moment before saying, "Eight should do it."

Paul checked his watch again: 3:47 A.M.

"You'll have to contact the others — Clay, Boulding," Pete went on. "And let Billings in Hong Kong know. He may still be at the office. And I guess you spoke to Ben."

"He's on his way home. I've left him a message."

"Good. See you at eight. Now, damn it, let me get some sleep."

Paul heard the line click dead. "Kill the messenger, why don't you," he muttered to himself. Sighing, he pressed the disconnect button for a dial tone.

First Clay, then Boulding, then Billings. It was a familiar litany by now. Just like that other litany — London, Frankfurt, Hong Kong, Tokyo, Chicago, Toronto, New York. The financial markets, an empire on which the sun never set. Paul yawned. He shifted his weight on the couch and began pressing the memorized numbers on the telephone's keypad.

One night, standing alone in the philosophical orange glow of the light above his kitchen sink, Paul had amused himself by trying to imagine the twistings and turnings of the great communications network he stood at the center of, waiting like an attentive spider for a tremor from some far corner of its global web. He imagined the thin copper wire — or fiber optic or whatever the hell they were using nowadays — leading from the end of his kitchen extension, spilling over the counter to the wall jack, where it connected up with a line that ran to the front of the house, to the outside wire slung over the front lawn, to the other wires that coursed along Grand Avenue, branching off east, west, north, south, feeding into the main lines, the switching stations, the transoceanic cables gnawed (if the *New York Times* was to be believed) by sharks. And then, at the other side of the ocean — in Brighton, Yokohama, Kowloon — the wire would emerge from the waves and reverse the process, telescoping down to main line, street line, house line, to the blunt, hairy hand of Derek Peabody, the graceful fingers of Kimiko Farley, the sweaty palm of Roger Billings or his daughter. It was an enormous electronic octopus, a worldwide nervous system (the metaphors kept coming to him), and he was at the heart of it all, information central, the control tower, ground zero. The thought had given him — as he stood there in the sweet specificity of his maroon-and-beige kitchen in the Hudson valley — a heady, ambiguous feeling, like the combination of confidence and insecurity one feels when climbing half drunk into the driver's seat of a car.

But now, as he made the required calls to Clay, Boulding, Billings — and then dropped the necessary E-mails and voice mails methodically into the boxes of everyone in the New York office — the only thing Paul felt was fatigue. It was already past four, and dawn was approaching invisibly from the east. Exhausted, he shuffled into the bedroom and quietly slipped under the covers next to Harriet. It felt good to be off his feet, off the telephone. The bed smelled wholesome and familiar, like warm grain. Harriet, rising a level or two from the depths of sleep, inhaled sharply and then rolled over toward him. Her hair seemed to be radiating heat. Paul angled his arm around her waist and closed his eyes. A fluid darkness seemed to swim beneath his eyelids. He told himself that he had two and a half hours ahead of him. Two and a half hours of oblivion.

He was almost asleep when he heard the little muffled cry from Donald's room next door.

"At least," Harriet said, changing Donald's diaper, "it's not as if your job is at stake." It was the next evening, after the meeting about the Renzer deal. Paul sat at the kitchen table watching his wife wrap the white Pamper around Donald's dimpled thigh, wondering idly if this — changing a diaper on the same surface that dinner had just been served on — was something that childless couples would find distressing. Donald, meanwhile, was staring up into the lights of the imitation-crystal chandelier, mesmerized. "Is it?"

Paul looked up suddenly. "What?"

"This deal," Harriet repeated, raising her thin, expressive eyebrows. "It's not as if your job is at stake, right?"

"Oh," Paul said. Then: "No, no, of course not." Paul had not slept in two days. After the 4 A.M. feeding that morning, Donald, ailing from what their insufferable pediatrician called "a frolic with colic," had been unable to get back to sleep. Paul had spent the rest of the night giving his son an in-depth tour of the living room, hoping to make him so bored that he'd drift off. But Donald had apparently found the living room interesting enough. So, when Harriet woke up at 6:30, Paul had simply handed the baby to her, showered, dressed, and driven over the bridge and down the highway to his office. By the time he arrived, Renzer had already fallen five and a quarter points in London. Pete Demiehl was furious. At the meeting, he shouted and sneered and seemed to hold Paul personally responsible for London's plummeting market. It was finally decided, after much discussion, that the deal with Renzer should be put on hold until the economic climate had stabilized.

"You would let me know, wouldn't you?" Harriet asked now. "It's just that I'd need a new outfit for bankruptcy court."

Paul smiled. "The markets are just a little shaky at this point," he said. "It'll be fine."

When the phone rang, Paul jumped up so fast that his head grazed the hanging crystals of the chandelier, causing Donald to gasp in approval. "Must be Tokyo," Paul said, but when he picked up the phone it was Ridgewood, New Jersey—Harriet's father. "So everybody's telling me it's time to bail out of the market," he began, without bothering to say hello.

"Hi, Pop," Paul said. He should have been expecting this, a communication from that other network of financial information in his life—Harriet's family. Harriet had an uncle who was a retired bond trader, two brothers in merchant banking, and a father who had his grandchildren's trust money (hard-earned during a blessed forty-three-year career as a housing contractor) invested in growth-oriented mutual funds. Every big rise and fall in the Dow Jones industrial average typically brought a flurry of phone calls from in-laws considering changes in their investment strategies. Somehow, despite the credentials of his wife's siblings, Paul was considered the family expert. Harriet said it was because he was so solid and upright, unlike her brothers, who reportedly played with money the way they used to play with stray cats—carelessly, ruthlessly, without regard for the sanctity of life.

"I keep thinking October '87," Pop went on. "So what do you think?"

"Hard to say. This is probably just a technical correction. The market has been due for a breather."

Harriet glanced over at Paul and made a face. She recognized his comment as an exact quote from the analyst they had just seen on the *Nightly Business Report*.

"Well, I'm nervous," Pop said then. "Don't you hotshots have software or something to let you know for sure? Special Internet tip-offs or whatever?"

"Yeah, Pop. There's this little farm up in Connecticut, and when the hens stop laying eggs, we know it's time to sell. But here's your no-good unemployed daughter, who's been waiting to talk to you all day." Paul quickly handed the phone to Harriet, who handed the baby to him. Donald looked up into his father's face with the same calm, all-accepting attention he had earlier given the chandelier. "Hi, Pop," Harriet said into the phone as Donald moved his lips.

Wearily, warily, Paul carried his son into the living room. He turned on the cable news and started pacing around the room. No, he assured himself, this couldn't affect his job. Paul took a deep, slow breath. He was feeling strange — bone-tired but restless. Too much caffeine, he guessed. His mind was speeding. He tried to concentrate on the television, where an unfamiliar anchorwoman was reporting about mounting tensions in some godforsaken place or other. A fat man came on after her and reported that a low-pressure system was approaching from the northwest. "And let's have another look at that wild day on Wall Street."

Paul sank into the armchair in front of the TV. Then he got up again. A low-pressure system. The Dow. He was a hopelessly entwined person, he told himself. He lived surrounded by complex, interrelated systems, magnifying every little disturbance, collecting the emitted impulses of an entire globe and focusing them on that little space halfway between his eyebrows and scalp line, where they pulsed and ached and wouldn't go away. Of course, it was that same sense of interconnection that had attracted him to finance in the first place — the continuousness of those systems, which made the market sensitive to everything from a corporate rumor to a tiny dip in interest rates. Plugging into that network was like playing a game with enormously convoluted rules that changed almost as quickly as they could be learned. He had loved playing that game. He still did love it, in fact. Only now he wished there was an off button somewhere. Now that he had a wife and child. Now that Renzer had fallen five and a quarter points in London.

All it would take, he told himself, would be a big drop in Hong Kong — call options would plummet, margin calls would be triggered, portfolios would collapse. A chain reaction, like the one that would follow the deceptive cloud on the radar screen, the button pressed, the silo in North Dakota opening, the needle-nosed missile maneuvering into position . . .

Oh, sure, sure, sure. Stop it, Paul told himself. He was tired. He wanted to rest. He wanted to look up into the spinning lights of a cheap chandelier and just be amused.

Paul found himself in the kitchen again just as Harriet was hanging up the phone. "Where's Donald?" she asked him.

Paul looked down. He wasn't carrying the baby anymore. He must have put him down somewhere. "Playpen," Paul guessed.

Harriet frowned. "When I go back to work," she said, sweeping past him, "we're going to redistribute the duties in this house."

Paul followed her into the flickering light of the living room. "I was up with him all last night, remember," he said. Harriet lifted Donald from the couch and hooked his chin over her shoulder. "And I'm afraid you'll be up with him again tonight," she said, beginning to pat his back. Paul only then noticed the wet gleam around her eyes. "My father didn't want to say anything to you before talking to me. He wants my brothers and me to go over there tonight. My great-aunt May is dying."

Paul got some sleep that night. Ben Farley called once, at 7:15 P.M., to tell him that Tokyo had stabilized nicely at the opening; Derek Peabody in London didn't call at all. Donald, meanwhile, woke only twice, at 12:45 and 4:10, and each time went right back to sleep after a warm bottle and a short, bouncy walk around the house. Paul slept — in the empty bed, alas — from 10:25 to 12:45, from 1:05 to 4:10, and from 4:30 until the alarm went off at 6:00.

He and Donald were already sitting in the kitchen, eating bananas for breakfast, when Harriet called to tell them that Aunt May had died. Paul winced, but of course they had all expected this news for some time; Aunt May's health had been deteriorating for months. But Paul could sense the upset in Harriet's voice. When she showed up about a half hour later, she looked foggy-eyed and pale, her dirtyish black hair pulled back in a sloppy braid. "May went quietly," she said, handing Paul the car keys. He was already late for work.

"Donald fell asleep playing in the laundry basket, so I left him there. And I've asked Judith to come over to watch him later so you can crash."

Harriet nodded and then tipped forward into his arms, pressing her check against his tie.

"She was old," Paul whispered to the top of her head.

"Oh, I know that," she answered. "I know it, I know it, I know it. It was just sitting there, though, in her bedroom, waiting. She was wearing all of her jewelry, everything — bracelets, rings, this old cameo my great-grandmother had given her. I didn't feel sad, exactly. I don't know. I felt alone. I missed my husband and baby."

Paul rubbed the back of her shoulders. "Get some sleep," he told her gently, his eye on the clock behind her.

Harriet's father had a heart attack at Aunt May's funeral. Paul and Harriet found out about it after the ceremony. Harriet's cousin Ruby told them, just as they were heading out toward the parking lot. During the eulogy, apparently, Pop had pulled Ruby's mother aside and told her that he was having chest pains. They were sitting in the back, where Pop always sat in any gathering, waiting to be of use: to turn up a thermostat or help the funeral director get the limos into place. He didn't want to disturb the ceremony, so the two of them had departed quietly for the hospital, leaving word with Ruby. Pop, it seemed, had forgotten his nitroglycerine tablets at home.

He had already been admitted by the time the family reached Englewood Hospital. The little blond martinet at the desk would allow only two visitors at a time, so Harriet's brothers offered to stay behind and let Harriet and Paul go up first. She agreed without another word, and the two of them pushed through the swinging glass doors into the ICU.

They found Pop lying in an elevated white bed, at the center of an intimidating tangle of hoses, wires, and tubes. He had an IV stuck into his hairy left arm, an oxygen tube taped under his nose, and various wires and electrodes running from his chest to three beeping and humming monitors that stood officiously around the room. Ruby's mother sat in a vinyl armchair next to the bed, holding Pop's hand. Both of them were grinning.

"You got nothing to worry about," Pop said to Harriet as they stepped into the room. "It was all over by the time we pulled into the emergency room." He took Harriet's head in one of his enormous hands and kissed her on the temple. "Now they got me all pumped up with nitro and I'm just fine, really. They're not even sure it was a real attack, per se. Bad angina, maybe. They just want to monitor me for a few days."

Harriet took his hand. "Damn you, Pop," she said. "This time I'm going to sew a packet of those damned pills into every shirt you own."

Pop chuckled, making the line on one of the monitor screens jump alarmingly. "Whatever you say, kid. Just don't worry."

Ruby's mother was watching him dreamily from her chair. "He was very brave," she said.

Harriet smiled uncertainly. "Anyway," she went on, "now that we know you're safe, we should tell Ron and Bill. They're downstairs waiting to hear."

"I'll go down," Paul offered, stepping up to the bed. "Glad you're okay, Pop."

"You!" Pop said, just now noticing Paul. "You, on the other hand, got something to worry about. Have you heard a news report lately? The market's crashing. I heard it on the car radio on the way in." He pulled his hand out of Harriet's and waved a gesture of disgust in Paul's direction. "The market's crashing, and taking my grandkids' trust funds with it!"

Ruby's mother clucked her tongue. Paul closed his eyes.

"This is not something a man in the process of a heart attack needs to hear," Pop said then, to his daughter.

Paul got home from the office at ten that night, while the Tokyo market was in midsession. Yes, the New York markets had been crashing as Pop spoke — the Dow down 424, the NASDAQ even worse — but stocks had recovered quickly from the breathtaking plunge. By the close, the Dow was down only 73 and change, while Tokyo had actually opened slightly higher. But Paul was still in a state of semishock. He had been swamped all day. Communications were down for minutes at a stretch. Pete Demiehl, looking ill, had called a meeting at 4:30 to try to pick up the pieces. The meeting had lasted until almost nine.

Harriet was in her flannel nightgown when Paul walked in. "Here," she said, handing Paul a big, comfortable mug of cocoa. "It'll relax us. We both need it."

Paul took off his tie and jacket and threw them unceremoniously behind the couch. "How's your father?"

"Depends on who you ask," Harriet said. She was standing in the kitchen doorway, leaning against the jamb in an unnatural way. "Pop says he's fine. Dr. Bernaducci is carefully noncommittal. He says Pop will be in intensive care for at least four days."

Paul nodded. "And Donald?"

"Sleeping like a baby."

Paul took a sip of his cocoa. He could feel the hot liquid spreading through his body. "Listen, I know it's your turn with him tonight," Paul said. "But I'll be up all night with this market thing anyway. There's no way I'll get any sleep."

Harriet came over behind the couch and started kneading the muscles in his neck. He put his head back against the warmth of her belly and closed his eyes. Little blue dots were flashing under his eyelids. He felt he could hear the fax machine in the laundry room bleating already.

"Scary," Harriet said, quietly, over his head. "You feel so vulnerable." Paul heard her breathe, and then, after a moment, she said, "I appreciate the offer. I'm worn out." She leaned over and pressed her lips against Paul's scalp. "The hospital says they'll call if there's any problem," she said, heading toward the bedroom. Then she stopped and turned around. "If you do get a chance to sleep at all, I'll be keeping it warm in there."

Paul watched her through the rising steam of his cocoa. "Do that. I'll disconnect the living room extension so you and Don won't be disturbed."

She nodded and shut the bedroom door gently behind her.

Paul was dozing, hours later, when the first call came. In his dream (searching for a path through rush-hour traffic, trying desperately to deliver something to a place he couldn't remember), he had identified the sound as the telephone. But as he came awake, he recognized it as Donald's telltale hungry squeal. Paul got up slowly from the couch. His watch read 4:13. He was amazed, and then worried, that he hadn't received any calls yet. Could there be something wrong with the telephone? He would check the fax and his E-mail after the bottle, check if anyone anywhere had left him a message.

He padded into Donald's room and lifted his son from the crib. Donald's cheeks sagged comically in the dim blue light. His oversized head seemed to sink down into the white softness of his shoulders. "Suppertime," Paul whispered to him. He put the baby over his shoulder and carried him out to the kitchen.

London called while he was warming up Donald's bottle. "It's looking bad," said Derek Peabody's voice. "Magnificently bad." Paul groaned while Derek told him exactly what he had been fearing and expecting — that the London and Frankfurt markets were crashing, that they were sinking even further and faster than in 1987.

"Oh God," Paul said, staring out the kitchen window at a haloed streetlight. Everything seemed perfectly normal out there. This was the way it happened now, Paul told himself. Disaster struck abstractly, announced by voices on a telephone, numbers on a screen — never seeming quite real. "Sounds pretty grim."

"Hey," Derek replied, "it's only the end of Western civilization as we know it. Anyway, my father always wanted me to join the family dry-cleaning business. 'Derek,' he'd say, 'whatever happens, the ladies of the world will always need clean blouses.'"

"Listen," Paul interrupted, "call me back when you hear something more. Whatever time, doesn't matter."

"You bet. Hang in there."

Paul hung up the phone. "Crashing," he said aloud to himself. It was such a strange word, he thought. So ambiguous. Crashing was what you did at a friend's house when your car wouldn't start. Crashing was what you did on the highway when your car did start. Paul thought suddenly of his dream about traffic, of rubber burning, and then realized that something smelled, something was burning. He ran over to the stove. The water he was using to warm the bottle had boiled away and now the plastic was melting in the pot. "Shit!" Paul flipped off the stove, grabbed the pot with one hand, and threw it into the sink. It hissed vigorously as he filled it with cold water from the tap. When the pot was full, he turned off the water. Little bits of charred plastic floated up in a roiling mixture of formula and water. Paul and Donald looked down at the mess in silence.

"So much for supper," Paul said into his son's ear. Then he swept Donald's tiny body over his head and held him toward the ceiling. His arms felt weak and unsteady. "London market's falling down, falling down, falling down." Donald slobbered delightedly as his father sang to him. "London market's falling down . . ."

The telephone rang. Paul stood there, staring at his son high above his head, as it rang five times, then eight, then ten. The phone finally stopped ringing. He lowered Donald to his shoulder. "My fair baby."

The telephone started ringing again. This was something important, Paul told himself as he walked over to the instrument. It was Hong Kong this time, or Frankfurt or Paris. Or maybe it was the Englewood Hospital, telling him that Pop was dead. Or his own sister, telling him of a brain tumor, a fire at his parents' house, a plane wreck. Paul could almost picture the next wave of calamity — the biggest and last, perhaps — building somewhere out in the distance, just out of sight. It was a matter of minutes until it hit. Or even seconds.

The telephone was still ringing. Paul knelt next to it. Calmly, deliberately, he pulled the telephone wire out of the modular jack in the wall.

He stood up again, the baby still clinging to his shoulder. He took a slow, agonizing breath. "No," he said aloud.

Then, imagining the storm of electronic impulses flashing around the thick shell of his house, he carried Donald into the master bedroom. He stood at the foot of his bed and took off his suit pants with one hand. Kicking them aside, he climbed into the gorgeous warmth of the bed. And there, with his son and his wife in his arms, he lay, patiently waiting for sleep.

from *Domestic Interior*

EAVAN BOLAND

Night Feed

This is dawn.
Believe me
This is your season, little daughter.
The moment daisies open,
The hour mercurial rainwater
Makes a mirror for sparrows.
It's time we drowned our sorrows.

I tiptoe in.
I lift you up
Wriggling
In your rosy, zipped sleeper.
Yes, this is the hour
For the early bird and me
When finder is keeper.

I crook the bottle.
How you suckle!
This is the best I can be,
Housewife
To this nursery
Where you hold on,
Dear life.

A silt of milk.
The last suck.
And now your eyes are open,
Birth-colored and offended.
Earth wakes.
You go back to sleep.
The feed is ended.

Worms turn.
Stars go in.
Even the moon is losing face.
Poplars stilt for dawn
And we begin
The long fall from grace.
I tuck you in.

Morning Song

SYLVIA PLATH

Love set you going like a fat gold watch.
The midwife slapped your footsoles, and your bald cry
Took its place among the elements.

Our voices echo, magnifying your arrival. New statue.
In a drafty museum, your nakedness
Shadows our safety. We stand round blankly as walls.

I'm no more your mother
Than the cloud that distills a mirror to reflect its own slow
Effacement at the wind's hand.

All night your moth-breath
Flickers among the flat pink roses. I wake to listen:
A far sea moves in my ear.

One cry, and I stumble from bed, cow-heavy and floral
In my Victorian nightgown.
Your mouth opens clean as a cat's. The window square

Whitens and swallows its dull stars. And now you try
Your handful of notes;
The clear vowels rise like balloons.

Sorrow

ANN TOWNSEND

It's in the air between us
as the next true moment
after I yell, tear sheets away,
spring from bed and you, faster,
grapple, wrestle me back
from the bedroom door.
Our hands slap at each other
as our *sorry, sorry* strikes the air.

The baby's furious wails
have penetrated even the earplugs
you wear to seal yourself
off at night, so you know
I hurry not to calm her, but to kill.
She's choked on a cough
so deep it blankets her lungs;
I'm shoving your hands away,

until at last we touch our own
nature, to go to her
with the false semblance of calm,
together, to boost her
to the window ledge
where the fat moon waits
like a white face
that cries from the deep black sky.

New Mother

SHARON OLDS

A week after our child was born,
you cornered me in the spare room
and we sank down on the bed.
You kissed me and kissed me, my milk undid its
burning slip-knot through my nipples,
soaking my shirt. All week I had smelled of milk,
fresh milk, sour. I began to throb:
my sex had been torn easily as cloth by the
crown of her head, I'd been cut with a knife and
sewn, the stitches pulling at my skin —
and the first time you're broken, you don't know
you'll be healed again, better than before.
I lay in fear and blood and milk
while you kissed and kissed me, your lips hot and swollen
as a teen-age boy's, your sex dry and big,
all of you so tender, you hung over me,
over the nest of stitches, over the
splitting and tearing, with the patience of someone who
finds a wounded animal in the woods
and stays with it, not leaving its side
until it is whole, until it can run again.

The Waiting

LI-YOUNG LEE

Now between your eyes
the furrows shine,
while your flushed
oval face floats
above the steaming
bath water.
Your shoulders roll, hips
sway side
to side,
legs stretch, rub together;
you call this luxury;
you pant a little;
your eyes close beneath
a thought. What, I wonder. Tonight
I'm saddened by those two
lines on your forehead,
by the knowledge
that each of their twins
lies here, between my own
eyes. Years
ago a man
and woman
quarrel,
waken their son. The woman runs
into the bedroom the three share and soothes him, while
in the other
room waits the man, who, if
he hears any
of what's going on

in the city —
traffic, the neighbor's TV, music
from an upstairs balcony,
his wife lilting
a child's tune — if he hears,
doesn't give it
away, this man
who one day
woke to find his life
hard, and who now
waits standing, too eager
to sit, the apartment too
small to pace, standing,
not to be caught
sitting in a life
toward which he came by device
and bad luck.
Her song ends, but she won't come, so he goes
in, to find
woman and child
asleep on the bed.
He lifts the small body
and lays him in his little bed by the wall.
He lies down by his wife.

I don't remember if he lay there remembering —
I hope he did, it
would have helped —
how they two, one year back, after hours
of rocking the child, an infant then,
began to make love,
and how the boy
wakened crying.
I hope

he closed his eyes to see
how the woman, naked, rose
to bring the baby to their bed, and, lying
with her back to the man,
suckled the boy while
the man lay longing, hard yet, thighs wet
from her, and on his chest
her odor.

By murmurs and thingless words
the mother answers
her son's sucking, his
gulping and mewling.
Rolling towards them, the man
reaches around her waist to stroke the boy's head.
Slowly, she reaches behind
and clasps him, fastens
him to her, while he
half mounts her damp length,
and spills his semen between her knees.
Exhausted, the three
bodies, complicated
thus, sleep a few hours,
until one rises
for work, in light
the color of breast milk drained on the sheet.

Love, these lines
accompany our want, nameless
or otherwise, and our waiting.
And since we've not learned
how not to want,
we've had to learn,

by waiting, how to wait.
So I wait
well, while you bathe.
Feet apart, you squat; shoulders stooped you reach
beneath to wash, and then I see
the mole on your right side, under your arm,
and I know—such knowledge
beautiful in its uselessness—
that it lies from your nipple
a distance precisely measured
by my left hand,
forefinger to wrist.
Now your legs fold
under, big slabs of water
slide up the tub
then down to clap
your hips and belly.
You sit atop your legs to wash your belly,
loose, soft from lately
birthing again, and streaked
with running milk, that pale fluid,
sweet, iron, astonishingly thin.

Ménage à trois

KATE DANIELS

Niobe keeps thinking of his eyes
inside her, before he was born. How large
they are, how brown. How their shape
is the shape of her eyes, and her mother's,
and others, far back, she never knew.
Niobe wonders what it felt like
to open them in there, the thick
and fecund liquid pressing all over.
The slow and downward drag
of those long lashes
and what it was he saw
inside her that he'll never tell,
that even his father will never know.
                                    And that

is what really thrills Niobe:
how different it is
between the father
and the son. How much
more intimate with the son.
And how this is the father's
greatest fear.

Breastfeeding in Indiana

JANE MCCAFFERTY

Two kinds of babies come into this world. You've probably met the first kind, whom I'll call "the easy babies," since that's what my mother calls them. "You sure didn't have easy babies," she says.

The easy babies are those generally peaceful creatures who "only cry when they're hungry or need to be changed," those babies whose mothers say, "Here, you want to hold her? She's not strange." These babies go with the flow. Their smiles are plentiful. If you needed to, you could prop them on your hip and teach a class. In the car, they babble happily or sleep. They love sleep. Why wouldn't they? They appreciate their soft cribs, their mobiles, the way the light flickers on the ceiling when the sun comes up. They really just *like* being babies.

Maybe you'll have a baby like this yourself. Some will suggest this stroke of luck is really your own doing: you were so calm during pregnancy; you fed the baby good vibes; you drank carrot juice and walked seven miles every morning. And your calming household, and you, and maybe your husband all are so nurturing and so full of good "energy" that your baby just soaked it up. I'm sure there's some truth in all that, but mostly everything's a mystery when you get down to it.

And besides, maybe you'll have the second kind of baby, whom I'll call "the wailers" which, given Bob Marley, is a much nicer term than "the difficult babies," which is what my mother calls them. The wailers can be born straight into a haven of deep peace and glowing warmth, yet still feel compelled to cry long and hard, in a variety of situations, as if communicating a complex story of passionate unhappiness that you will never understand. Change their diapers, feed them, rock them, sing to them, take them out to see the stars. Go ahead, something might work. But at times the wailers will go on wailing, no matter what you do. And sometimes these babies may get especially uncomfortable in the car.

My first daughter, born wailer, was constitutionally opposed to travel by car, and had been since she was ten days old, when I'd tried to take her two blocks away to the Giant Eagle grocery store. I don't know if it was the movement of the car or being strapped like an astronaut into her car seat that so enraged and frightened her. Maybe she just didn't get the point of it. I tried to see it from her point of view: let's see, they strap me into an oddly angled seat in a small, boring room where for some reason we all sit still and face in the same direction. After an interminable amount of time they lift me out. (Think about it: a baby doesn't understand the notion of *going somewhere*.) So maybe the seeming pointlessness of it all made her cry?

Others who had crying babies claimed that a little trip in the car just knocked them right out. "Straight to dreamland," they said. "It's like a miracle cure."

"But our baby *hates* the car."

"Oh! Then put her on the dryer, turn the dryer on, see how that works, or turn the shower on and stand in the bathroom with her! The shower trick gets 'em every time. Or just put the baby in the sink and then blare music in the next room. Babies really like Springsteen, in fact ours loves *The Wild, the Innocent and the E Street Shuffle*, but it has to be in the next room, and they like it when they're warm and wet in the sink, so . . ."

Didn't these exuberant advice givers (you'll meet them) understand that as Americans we needed sometimes to be in the car and that we didn't have a dryer or a shower in our car, much less a sink and a next room? In fact we didn't even have a tiny TV or computer in our car. We believed a car was sacred space to be protected from all technology other than our cassette player, which still worked back then, but even her favorite Nigerian lullaby, "Abi yo yo," made her howl when we were moving.

Sometimes I would try to go out with my friend Jennifer and her baby Aryeh, who was exactly my daughter's age. We'd plan a car trip to Pittsburgh's toy-lending library. I can still see the two babies strapped into their car seats side by side in the backseat of my car, Aryeh like the Buddha, my daughter like the guy in the Munch painting. She'd get louder and fiercer.

Jennifer would look at me with considerable pity. Aryeh would sometimes join my daughter, but his were squeaky little tears of empathy. "Um, maybe we can go tomorrow? And you can like, drop us off here?" Jennifer would suggest.

"We love to walk, and it's so pretty outside." "Sure, sure, I understand," I'd say, looking out at the thick, dark winter sky. She'd walk away with her blue-eyed Buddha. He was bottle-fed, and I think I'd put all her fears to rest about that; Rosey was breastfed and look at her!

I'd hurry us home. And what I remember most is how I never once thought, "I wish Rosemary could be more like Aryeh." You'll fall so crazily in love with your own baby! Much more than you could ever imagine. For the few months before I gave birth, I was afraid that I could never love my baby as much as I already loved my two stepsons Josh and Jordan. This is a common feeling for all parents who already have children they love, no matter how they acquire them. As it turned out, I fell so hard and deep for Rosemary I actually felt a little bit sorry for all my friends who had babies that weren't her. Surely they could see she was the greatest baby on earth. Surely they felt a few pangs of envy when they laid eyes upon her.

My husband and I, already inclined toward believing that we understood very little about anything, began to believe a little bit more in past lives as a result of Rosemary's extreme car aversion. Her previous life had probably ended in a car wreck, we decided, even though she'd been wearing her seat belt. She was so persistently, piercingly, vocal we also decided that she might just have been either a gym teacher (in an unruly Catholic school) or a diva, or some combination of the two.

One May day my husband drove us to the planet of the Midwest, for a family celebration. We made it fifteen minutes down the road from Pittsburgh before we had to stop to calm her. It was going to be a long trip. On a good day, with no babies, it would be seven hours. At this rate we would get there next Wednesday. We would miss his great-grandparents' fiftieth wedding anniversary party. And that's why we were doing this. That's why we were now parked in front of an auto shop, unstrapping the reluctant astronaut, whose crying ceased just as soon as you lifted her out of the seat. Now we walked in the May sunlight of the lot together, and she was wide-eyed, her little head under my chin, her sweet baby smell the smell of endless forgiveness. My husband with rattled nerves sat in the driver's seat, head down on the wheel. Most men have a much harder time listening to a baby cry than women do. He is like that, only more so, and he was worn out right here at the beginning of our trip. And the poor guy couldn't breastfeed, which is what I was doing now, to get her to sleep.

I sat in the backseat and fed her, and he got the lullaby tape ready, and then somehow I managed to place her in the seat without her waking. My husband started the car and still she did not stir. Few moments in life are as victorious as those that follow the ones where you've just put the baby to sleep. We traveled in peace and late sunlight listening to those lullabies for almost an hour before she piped up again. "We really can't stop," my husband said. "No, we can't," I said. And this necessity of having to hurtle ourselves toward a fiftieth anniversary party had me discover the old breastfeeding-while-baby-is-in-car-seat-and-car-is-roaring-toward-the-Midwest-at-seventy-m.p.h. trick.

There's a fair chance you might need this trick. So. First, stand up in your hunchback position and face the baby. Now hunch down further, until somehow your breasts are aligned in the general direction of your baby's mouth. Now take one breast out of your nursing bra, move the breast toward the baby, and even though you're really quite contorted at this point, leaning sideways, neck craned so that you'll need a massage you won't get later, it'll be worth it because usually the little one will stop to drink. Aching, twisted into a bizarre and punishing shape, you'll be happy, and your husband will think you're a hero, which you are in this little microcosm. "I don't know how you do it," my husband always said, sweet and generous with praise. "Thank you," I said. But I loved it. She was my first baby! I was the most useful body on earth, a fountain of sweetness. Pain was nothing in the face of the joy she'd ushered in by being born! I mean it, I'm remembering this accurately. I was ecstatic to be contorted like that, and we didn't make another stop for over two hours! Every time she stirred she got the breast.

I admit the trick has its limits. You could do permanent damage to your spine, for instance. But finally the babies will cry vociferously, and wag their heads to tell you the breast is getting tiresome.

It was dark by this time. We'd made it into Ohio. I was trying to sing "Love Grows Where My Rosemary Goes." We pulled over in a field on the freeway's edge, but you could smell Toledo looming up at the next exit. "Should we take a break in Toledo? Get a cup of coffee?" my husband said.

"Coffee! I can't drink coffee!"

"You know what I mean."

"No. No stopping in Toledo. We must push forward!"

"Are you sure you're ok?"

"Yes!"

"You're amazing back there."

"Yes!"

We played with her in the freeway field, far away as possible from the bru-
tality of the cars. How terribly big and loud they will seem when you have such
innocence and fragility in your arms. Why don't they have special designated
places for infants every thirty miles or so? If we really liked babies in this culture, a rest stop would include a hushed environment of color and soft objects
and books you can bite. The back porch of the hushed environment would
lead to a field of wildflowers, a deer in the distance, several swings would hang
from a series of old oak trees, yes, a grove, where all the frazzled parents sit
swinging gently in the silence with their babies on their laps.

Anyhow, we finally arrived at my mother-in-law's. Though it was near midnight, no welcoming face could be brighter than hers at the door awaiting a
chance to hold her granddaughter. We were exhausted, but lucky to be in her
country living room where she demanded nothing of you. She held the baby
and rocked her and listened to our bizarre story of traveling all day. She was
too far removed from motherhood to try to give us advice. She just shook her
head in a kind of astonished sympathy. She didn't have that look of suspicion
on her face that some relatives had when hearing of such adventures: a look
that means, "If you'd give her normal food, you wouldn't have this problem,"
or "If she slept in her own crib and not with you, you wouldn't have this problem," or "If you played American lullabies and not those damn foreign things,
you wouldn't have this problem." No, my mother-in-law has the kind of wisdom that is partly the result of having had her own *four* babies by the time she
turned twenty-one. (I'd nearly driven her crazy when I was pregnant and ob-
sessed with my diet. I had a panic attack when I ate a cup of yogurt at her
house once, because *What to Expect When You're Expecting* had said something about how yogurt can sit on trucks unrefrigerated, and this lack of cold

air turns yogurt into a poison that could cause birth defects. "I have to make myself throw up!" I cried with a passion I hadn't felt since I was a fervent little Catholic eight-year-old who'd devoured a Slim-Jim on Good Friday.) My own mother had smoked and drank when she was pregnant, and my mother-in-law had probably survived on candy and hamburger meat, so you can imagine I seemed crazy to both of them, and you will, too, if you go this route, which you probably will if someone buys you *What to Expect*, which they probably will.

So the next day we go to Fort Wayne, Indiana, where my husband's great-grandparents have lived in a tiny ranch for all their adult lives, a ranch where nothing has ever changed (except for the additions of photos of grandchildren and great-grandchildren) or been redecorated, where his great-grandmother, a tall, lovely white-haired woman will always sit you at her kitchen table and feed you ham salad with thickly, and I mean *thickly*, buttered bread, and my husband's great-grandfather will show you his meticulous garden and tell you some off-color jokes.

For this particular visit, Great-Grandma sat on the floor holding the baby, who smiled at her. Like all babies, Rosemary had a smile more devastating than you could ever be prepared for. We visited, we sat on the stiff couch and marveled at the still-life that is their house, and then I believe it grew late and we caravanned over to the Oak Grove Inn, where the big party would be held.

It was in the basement of this nice old restaurant, the kind of place old people go on Sundays, and indeed the fortunate couple had frequented the place for fifty years. A lush buffet of meat and thoroughly cooked vegetables was set up under sturdy metal lids, along with pies and whipped cream. I had a root beer and this felt a little racy, since what nutritional value for the baby did root beer have? It was the first time in a year I'd ingested something that wasn't a vitamin or calcium source. The aunts and cousins and uncles enjoyed themselves at the tables, slowly sipping whiskey sours or wine, in a way that always strikes me as Protestant. It was very loud. I can't remember if it was music that made the noise, or just the crowd. Some folks, as they call people in the Midwest (very presidential of them we see now), were smoking. I'm no smoke snob; I had the bad habit myself from age 13 to 28. However, when you have this baby in your arms whose lungs are more pure than the innermost petals of a rose, you don't want to be in a room that's getting hazy with expelled clouds of nicotine. Who was the man who came over to me and blew smoke in the baby's face as a little experiment? I think his name was Luther. I managed to turn her away so that most of it didn't get to her. But I really wanted to knock Luther on his ass. The better part of me knew he was a well-meaning fool and not a sadist, so I just rose up those steps holding my tongue and temper and kissing her head. If this happens to you, just remember, one day the image of smoke in your baby's face will hardly affect you at all, much less feel like a violent invasion. With just a little luck, your baby will soon (too soon) become a kid with a fashionable lunchbox, waving goodbye as she gallops toward the bus, just as Rosemary did this morning.

But that night, seven years ago, she'd only been on this earth for three months. Upstairs, just one floor removed from the special-events basement, was the regular restaurant. The basement had been close, sticky, full of the well-meaning sweat of humanity. Outside it was humid, summer moving in too quickly. But in the restaurant itself, the air was cool and dark, and I moved into it as if greeting my old best friend, the one who always understood when I needed some space. Business was not booming here. The tables were empty except for a few older couples seated on the far side of the room, no doubt eating fried and breaded fish or ham. No doubt enjoying some ritualized talk, or silence, along with that sense of being citizens of the heartland.

"Can I just sit down here a while?" I asked the hostess. She smiled and looked around the room, as if to see if the manager was available. "I'll just sit and be quiet, it's too smoky downstairs, I'm with the party below us—"

"I don't see any harm in it," she said. "Go on and sit down over there."

I sat and discreetly began to feed the baby, my back turned to the customers. I had on a nursing shirt—the kind that have windows you can unsnap. And of course the elegant nursing bra, too, so it wasn't like this was difficult for me. Besides, I'd nursed everywhere, including K-Mart and church.

I ordered a glass of water. I was always thirsty, and now after that sinful root beer I was really parched, and I wanted to dilute the root beer so the baby would get less sugar. In fact, I was feeling pretty bad about that root beer, if you can believe that. But the baby drank eagerly, and I relaxed. I could hear the party below, and I loved the feeling of wishing them all well from this quiet distance. I wouldn't be answering any questions for a while, such as "Now where did she get all that hair?" and "Is she on a schedule?" and "Does she look a little like Uncle Harry?" though I never minded those questions too much. Remember, babies obliterate you for a while. All conversations will center around baby. Enjoy this. Revel in your own obliteration. It's really a vacation. A great big part of you—a whole gang of the selves you usually have to be—is simply out to lunch. Let the gang be.

That evening in the restaurant, I felt such simple relief, pleasure, and gratitude, just to be feeding my child. I liked breastfeeding. Anything that brought me closer to animals (except for things like mauling) was a good thing, and motherhood will do that whether you breastfeed or not. I know some of you out there will like breastfeeding even more than I did. Some will even be orgasmic; in fact I heard once on a radio talk show that a small percentage of women *regularly* have orgasms when breastfeeding. More power to them, but if you're one of them, and you end up in the Oak Grove Inn with some folks, try to control yourself, ok?

I was so relaxed there, sipping water while the baby nursed. I felt I could curl up like a bear in a cave with this cub. But the waitress was coming my way, and yes, coming my way indeed, she looked a little *urgent*, a little uncomfortable, and she leaned over and said to me, "Um, you have to stop doing that, a customer complained."

"Doing what?" I said, not meaning to be obtuse.

"Um, with your baby." (In Indiana they talk a lot like the people in *Fargo* so you'll have to supply the accent in your mind.)

"Breastfeeding?"

"Um, yes, that's right."

"A customer complained?"

"Yes."

"Which one?"

But I had turned in my seat, and it was obvious which one. The woman in the corner was *tsking*. I hadn't heard tsking in so long. And maybe never, maybe I'd only read about tsking in books. To accompany the tsk she wagged her head. She was an older woman dining with what appeared to be a husband and an adult child. I waved. She shook her head with a firm straight mouth, as if to say, "Don't think you can win me over, missy."

"She said you were breaking the law," said the waitress, who seemed a little dim and confused.

"Breaking the law." I imbued my voice with a sarcasm that seemed completely foreign in that place.

"That's right," she said, perkily. "And she said she would tell the owner about this."

"The owner," I said, nodding to put the waitress at ease. "I understand."

But our interaction was taking too long.

"We are trying to eat our supper over here!" the woman called over.

"So was my baby!" I called back. "Is that against the damn law?"

I stood up. She said it figured I would use foul language.

Enraged, I took my baby outside into the warmth of the evening. I was speechless now, pacing, then finally settling down to feed Rosey on a patch of grass. Together we were animals again.

I paced thinking how I really wished I'd made a better exit. I could've said, "Thanks for the old-fashioned midwestern hospitality, ya fuckers!" (Never would I have said it, but it helped to imagine it as I paced with my crying infant.) I could've ripped off my shirt and walked up to her table topless and faced down her disgust. (This, too, was wonderful to imagine.) I know women wild enough to do this. Maybe you will be one.

But understand, this poor woman's bones had been glutted with Calvinism. Her very breath had been singed with shame. She hated her body, and always had, like so many women do. She'd been taught well, and learned quickly and deeply. And she hated my body because it was like a memory of hers. She hated the thirsty baby, because she was so thirsty herself.

Maybe she was young in front of an old dresser mirror once. Maybe she couldn't help but touch her body when she was pregnant that time. If you were wild enough to rip your shirt off and face down her disgust, she would hate you initially, but then she'd probably have a dream, where your face blurred into hers. She would remember that old dresser mirror, herself swimming in it on a perfect autumn day when she was seven months pregnant. She ran her hands over her belly, her breasts, outside of time for that one moment, before the tree beyond the window shook its limb, lowered its brow. But just maybe in the dream the tree will be golden red and shimmering, the applause of the leaves running up and down her body, the first drop of milk shining like a tiny moon on the new world of her dark nipple.

Today, with four children—two daughters I gave birth to and two high school stepsons I've helped raise since they were three and five years old—I'd like to find that old woman somehow, and take a walk with her down some lost Indiana back road that she knows by heart. I'd like to ask her to tell me the story of herself as a new mother (Did she have an easy baby or a wailer?) and how she fed those she loved. (Did she breastfeed alone in a room with the door locked? Did she not breastfeed at all? Did the formula salesmen really come right into the maternity ward the way I've heard?) And how did she and didn't she feed herself. (Was there something secret she loved to do that was all her own? Paint? Ice-skate? Run like a girl with the family dog?)

And then I'd ask her how it really feels, when you're near the end of your life, to remember how it felt to hold your first baby in your arms.

"Tell me you don't ever forget," I'd say.

Her eyes would shine with longing. "You never forget," she'd say. "Never."

March

JIM DANIELS

My parents just left after a surprise
visit — a baby fix with my new child.

My shoes are muddy from a tromp in the yard —
I stepped on some tulips, clumsy for spring.

I plunged a shovel into wet dirt, digging
for a heart. I wipe my shoes in the last

of the snow. I need a haircut. I need grass seed.
My parents drive on the freeway toward home,

my old home. Where will they stop for lunch?
Denny's? Big Boy's? I change their sheets.

I hold them to my face. My father offered
to cut my hair. It's a joke between us.

He cuts my grandfather's hair, the only person
who'll still let him. Once you hit ninety,

I guess you don't care. I cut some pussy willows
and put them in a vase. I rub the fuzz against

my cheek. I made my last snowball and threw it
at my father's car, a joke between us. The kid,

he's taking a nap. I've been trying not
to mention him, the invisible spine.

I'll show him the pussy willows and see
if he laughs. He hasn't had a haircut yet.

I'll see if he cries — one more new thing
in this world. My aging parents have skin problems.

My mother uses Superglue to heal the cracks.
My father uses this stuff called Nu-Skin.

He says he can't bowl without it.
He uses the same ball I used to sit on

in the closet where I stretched
the phone cord for privacy with my girlfriend.

What did I say sitting there in the dark?
I probably said *I love you forever.*

What did I know? My muddy footprints
in the end of the snow, melting.

First Summer

LAURIE KUTCHINS

The first time I felt like a mother
it was summer, almost the solstice,
and I had been alone with him
for weeks, lulled into walking
by evening light, still trying
to preserve the dissolving shape
of my former life. Everything I was
was abruptly funneled into infant time:
the unstructured rounds of nursing
and napping, the lamb-like cries
pulling me out of dreamless,
snatched sleeps; the firm gums
wandering from one hill of milk
to the other, small teeth already made
and hidden inside; the eyes still filled
with that other world, unable to find me
across a room; the hand washes
of that tiny miraculous penis;
the sleepers and burper rags; the smell
of his head where light entered
through the sponge of the fontanelle.
Time wove around us an indelible gauze
like mosquito netting, tedious
yet blessed.
     Storms and clearings.
I bundled him in layers of cloth,
tucked him in the soft pack across my chest,
steadied his head in my palm
like a warmed teacup.

In the dusk, our walking shadow loomed
a long-legged, pregnant shape,
then fell into the hill as we neared the rise.
Catching his scent, the wind sniffed
the new skin and human milk
of him, and came closer.

The sun dropped into the dark ruffle
of mountains as if the earth had swallowed it.
At that moment the wind lunged, a vehement rush,
forced its way down his thin windpipe.
He awoke, jerked back at the neck, swayed
by a gravity greater than the world
of my body. His eyes
widened and bulged, still tearless,
centering me in their fear.
I watched what was invisible
take him with the force
of a swollen current, jaws clenched
and unclenched, I heard the first gasp
of his voice, the cold sleet wind
clutching his delicate throat, an animal
I could not chase away, a spirit
I could not pull back out of him.

Only weeks earlier, in the first tides
of exhaustion, milk, and loss,
I'd flung him sweaty one night
from my arms onto the bed, clasped my hands
behind my neck, gnashed my teeth, and fought off
a fantasy of infanticide, an urge
to take the pillow and squelch

the breath in him, how swift and effortless
I could have done it,
breath my body had labored
to separate from me.
How do I claim that memory, connect
that moment with dusk on the hill-rise
when the wind overcame him
and I rose up with the immense power of a Kali,
of Demeter,
and cupped my hands around his mouth
and turned my back to the wind I love, its darkness,
to make a human windbreak,
to keep a small flame going?

Now That I Am
Forever with Child

Little Sleep's-Head Sprouting Hair in the Moonlight

GALWAY KINNELL

1

You cry, waking from a nightmare.

When I sleepwalk
into your room, and pick you up,
and hold you up in the moonlight, you cling to me
hard,
as if clinging could save us. I think
you think
I will never die, I think I exude
to you the permanence of smoke or stars,
even as
my broken arms heal themselves around you.

2

I have heard you tell
the sun, *don't go down*, I have stood by
as you told the flower, *don't grow old,*
don't die. Little Maud,

I would blow the flame out of your silver cup,
I would suck the rot from your fingernail,
I would brush your sprouting hair of the dying light,
I would scrape the rust off your ivory bones,
I would help death escape through the little ribs of your body,
I would alchemize the ashes of your cradle back into wood,
I would let nothing of you go, ever,

until washerwomen
feel the clothes fall asleep in their hands,
and hens scratch their spell across hatchet blades,
and rats walk away from the cultures of the plague,
and iron twists weapons toward the true north,
and grease refuses to slide in the machinery of progress,
and men feel as free on earth as fleas on the bodies of men,
and lovers no longer whisper to the one beside them in the
　　dark, O *you-who-will-no-longer-be* . . .

And yet perhaps this is the reason you cry,
this the nightmare you wake crying from:
being forever
in the pre-trembling of a house that falls.

3

In a restaurant once, everyone
quietly eating, you clambered up
on my lap: to all
the mouthfuls rising toward
all the mouths, at the top of your voice
you cried
your one word, *caca! caca! caca!*
and each spoonful
stopped, a moment, in midair, in its withering
steam.

Yes,
you cling because
I, like you, only sooner
than you, will go down
the path of vanished alphabets,
the roadlessness
to the other side of the darkness,
your arms
like the shoes left behind,
like the adjectives in the halting speech
of very old men,
which used to be able to call up the forgotten nouns.

4

And you yourself,
some impossible Tuesday
in the year Two Thousand and Nine, will walk out
among the black stones
of the field, in the rain,
and the stones saying
over their one word, *ci-gît, ci-gît, ci-gît,*

and the raindrops
hitting you on the fontanel
over and over, and you standing there
unable to let them in.

5

If one day it happens
you find yourself with someone you love
in a café at one end
of the Pont Mirabeau, at the zinc bar
where white wine stands in upward opening glasses,

and if you commit then, as we did, the error
of thinking,
one day all this will only be memory,

learn to reach deeper
into the sorrows
to come — to touch
the almost imaginary bones
under the face, to hear under the laughter
the wind crying across the stones. Kiss
the mouth
which tells you, *here*,
here is the world. This mouth. This laughter. These temple bones.

The still undanced cadence of vanishing.

6

In the light the moon
sends back, I can see in your eyes

the hand that waved once
in my father's eyes, a tiny kite
wobbling far up in the twilight of his last look,
and the angel
of all mortal things lets go the string.

7

Back you go, into your crib.
The last blackbird lights up his gold wings: *farewell*.
Your eyes close inside your head,
in sleep. Already
in your dreams the hours begin to sing.

Little sleep's-head sprouting hair in the moonlight,
when I come back
we will go out together,
we will walk out together among
the ten thousand things,
each scratched in time with such knowledge, *the wages
of dying is love.*

Brown Circle

LOUISE GLÜCK

My mother wants to know
why, if I hate
family so much,
I went ahead and
had one. I don't
answer my mother.
What I hated
was being a child,
having no choice about
what people I loved.

I don't love my son
the way I meant to love him.
I thought I'd be
the lover of orchids who finds
red trillium growing
in the pine shades, and doesn't
touch it, doesn't need
to possess it. What I am
is the scientist,
who comes to that flower
with a magnifying glass
and doesn't leave, though
the sun burns a brown
circle of grass around
the flower. Which is
more or less the way
my mother loved me.

I must learn
to forgive my mother,
now that I'm helpless
to spare my son.

Simple Joys

QUINCY TROUPE

my young son, porter, watching snowflakes
whoops, in ecstasy, as they collect, like lint,
on the front windshield of my car, his growing
hands try to snag them through the tinted glass
as they hit & melt, like dead faces time erases
in a flash, though he misses & leaves only his
handprints on the tinted glass, there, his sudden
simple joy of discovering, suddenly, switches
like the attention span of television,
his eyes now locked onto spinning car wheels
churning in surprise, his imagination scotchtaping
itself to everything, tripping over everything, turning
snowflakes into flowers, brown brushstrokes stroking
the windshield become the tail of our cat, tchikaya,
window bars, baseball bats in the eyes of his dazzling
invention, wonder resides there, like magic,
everyday the curtain goes up on his transforming
pure eyes, that see metaphors everywhere
& it gives me sweet joy in this age of cynicism
to watch & be with him tripping through discovery —
his simple joys the envy of my caged wisdom

Motherhood

RITA DOVE

She dreams the baby's so small she keeps
misplacing it — it rolls from the hutch
and the mouse carries it home, it disappears
with his shirt in the wash.
Then she drops it and it explodes
like a watermelon, eyes spitting.

Finally they get to the countryside;
Thomas has it in a sling.
He's strewing rice along the road
while the trees chitter with tiny birds.
In the meadow to their right three men
are playing rough with a white wolf. She calls

warning but the wolf breaks free
and she runs, the rattle
rolls into the gully, then she's
there and tossing the baby behind her,
listening for its cry as she straddles
the wolf and circles its throat, counting
until her thumbs push through to the earth.
White fur seeps red. She is hardly breathing.
The small wild eyes
go opaque with confusion and shame, like a child's.

Propaganda Poem: Maybe for Some Young Mamas

ALICIA OSTRIKER

1. The Visiting Poet

> (after reading the girls my old pregnancy poem
> that I thought ripe and beautiful
> after they made themselves clear it was ugly
> after telling the girls I would as soon
> go to my grave a virgin, god
> forbid, as go to my grave without
> ever bearing and rearing a child
> I laughed
> and if looks could kill I would
> have been one dead duck in that
> so-called "feminist" classroom)

Oh young girls in a classroom
with your smooth skins like paper not yet written on
your good American bodies, your breasts, your bellies
fed healthy on hamburgers and milkshakes, almost
like photographs in solution half-developed
I leaned and strained toward you, trying to understand
what you were becoming
as you sat so quietly under the winter light
that fell into our classroom
and I tried, as a teacher, to transmit information
that's my job, knowledge like currency
you have to spend it

oh young mamas
no matter what your age is you

are born when you give birth
to a baby you start over

one animal

and both gently just slightly
separated from each other
swaying, swinging
like a vine, like an oriole nest
keep returning to each other
like a little tide, like a little wave
for a little while
    better than sex, that bitter honey, maybe
    could be the connection you've been waiting for
    because no man is god, no woman is a goddess
    we are all of us spoiled by that time

    but a baby
      any baby
        your baby is
          the
    most perfect human thing you can ever touch
    translucent
    and I want you to think about touching
    and the pleasure of touching
    and being touched by this most perfect thing
      this pear tree blossom
     this mouth these leafy hands these genitals
      like petals
    a warm scalp resting against your cheek
      fruit's warmth
      beginning —

Curtains curtains you say young girls
we want to live our lives
don't want the burden the responsibility
the disgusting mess
of children
we want our freedom and we want it now
I see you shudder truly and I wonder what
                    kind of lives you want so badly
                    to live or who has cut you with what axes
                    from the sense of your
                    flowing sap or why
                    are you made of sand
young girls will you walk
out of this door and spend your substance freely
or who has shown to you the greedy mirror
the lying mirror
the desert
sand —

I am telling you and you can take me for a fool there is no
good time like the good time a whole mama
has with a whole little baby and that's
                    where the first images
of deity came from — sister you know it's true
you know in secret how they
cut us down
                    because who can bear the joy that hurts nobody
                    the dazzling circuit of contact without dominance
                    that by the way might make you less vulnerable
                    to cancer and who knows what other diseases
                    of the body

because who can bear a thing that makes you happy
and rolls the world a little way
on forward
toward its destiny

because a woman is acceptable if she is
weak
acceptable if she is a victim
acceptable also if she is an angry victim ("shrew," "witch")
a woman's sorrow is acceptable
a deodorized sanitized sterilized antiperspirant
grinning efficient woman is certainly acceptable

but who can tolerate the power of a woman
close to a child, riding our tides
into the sand dunes of the public spaces.

2. *Postscript to Propaganda*

That they limit your liberty, of course,
entirely. That they limit your cash. That they limit your sleep.
Your sleep is a dirty torn cloth.
That they whine until you want to murder them. That their beauty
prevents you. That their eating and excreting exactly resembles
the slime-trails of slugs. On your knees you follow, cleaning,
unstaining. That they burn themselves, lacerate themselves, bruise
themselves. That they get ill. That you sit at their bedsides
exhausted, coughing, reading dully to them, wiping their foreheads
with wet washcloths to lower the fever, your life peeling away
from you like layers of cellophane. Of course.

That you are wheels to them. That you are grease.
An iron doorway they kick open, they run out, nobody has
remembered to close it. That their demanding is a grey north wind.
That their sullenness is a damp that rots your wood, their
malice a metal that draws your blood, their disobedience the fire that
burns your sacred book, their sorrows the webbing that entraps you
like a thrashing fish. That when your child grieves, mother,
you bend and grieve. That you disentwine yourself from them, lock
the pores of your love, set them at a distance. That in this
fashion the years pass, like calendar pages flipped in a silent
movie, and you are old, you are wrinkled as tortoises.

Come on, you daughters of bitches, do you want to live forever?

   3. *What Actually*

What a lot of garbage we all shovel. What a lot of
self-serving, self-pitying rhetoric we splash around in.
We paint ourselves wrong. How can I, to paraphrase the
poet, say what I actually mean? What, anyway, do I mean?
About motherhood? It is the unanimity that offends me.
The ideological lockstep, that cannot permit women, humans,
simply to choose for themselves. When I was in college
everyone expected to get married and have babies, and
everyone thought this was her own idea, although from this
distance we can see that we were programmed. Presently
everyone believes motherhood is the sinister invention
of patriarchy.

This week in Paris I learned that the serious intellectual
women are into lesbianism, incest, armed violence and the
theory of hysteria. G. gave her slide lecture on the
re-emergence of the goddess image in women's art and was
called a Nazi. How can I be a Nazi, she said, I'm a Jew.

A friend's daughter dies of crib death. She tries to have
another, fails. Fails. Fails. She and her husband divorce,
she moves to another town, in a year she is pregnant. She
does not want to marry the nice young man. She does not
want an abortion. She keeps her job, she has the baby, she
prays. A friend crosses her fifty-year-old legs in bluejeans,
swallows her vodka and says she knows that nothing but her
sobbing when at last she was alone in the airport parking lot
kept her children's jet from crashing in the Atlantic. A
friend's green-eyed son has leukemia, he plays baseball, he
collects stamps, she buys a camera and takes pictures of him
in teeshirt and shorts, as naked as she dares.

Born. I believe that some of us are born to be mamas,
nobody can know how many or which ones. We are probably
identifiable at an early age by our foolish happiness in the
presence of smaller children. Some born not to be. Some in
the middle. Were there maybe a few young mamas sitting in
that classroom in the winter light, subdued, their codes
inaudible? Were they afraid to choose? Have we not explained
to the young that choice equals risk? Wanted to tell them to
decode themselves, like unwrapping a package carefully, not to
damage it. Wanted to tell them, mamas or not mamas, we all get
damaged when put to use, we get like wornout houses, but only
the life that hoards and coffins itself is already dead.

Saul and Patsy Are in Labor

CHARLES BAXTER

The moonlight on the sheets is as heavy as damp cotton, and Patsy, pregnant in her ninth month with a child who does not care to be born, sits up in bed to glare at whatever is still visible. The moonlight falls on the red oak bedroom floor, the carved polar bear on the bedside table, and her husband, Saul, under his electric blanket. Sleeping, Saul is always cold. His dreams, he has reported, are Arctic. Moonlit, he seems a bit blue. But it soothes her, having him there: his quiet groans and his exhaling supply the rhythms of Patsy's waking nights.

She pulls back the covers, walks to the window, and sheds her nightgown.

Brown-haired, athletic, with a runner's body, she is ordinarily a slender woman, but now her breasts and belly are swollen, the skin stretched taut, her fingers and feet thickened with water. She finds herself tilting backward to balance herself against her new frontal weight. She feels like a human rain forest: hot, choked with life, reeking with reproduction.

Out in the yard the full-faced moon shines through two pine trees this side of the garage and on Saul's motorcycle parked in the driveway. Beyond the garage she sees a single deer passing silently through the field.

Patsy leans toward the desk in front of the window and permits the moon to gaze on her nakedness. She soaks up the moonlight, bathes in it. As she turns, she clasps her hands behind her head. She's had it with pregnancy; now she wants the labor, the full-blast finality of it. When she looks at the desk she sees the ampersand key on the upper row of the typewriter keyboard, the & above the 7. It's shaped like herself, distended and full: the big female *and*: &. The baby gives her a sleepy kick.

Hey, she says to the moonlight, *put me in labor. Pull this child into the world. Help me out here.*

Three hours later, just before dawn, her water breaks.

The labor room: Between contractions and the blips of the fetal monitor, she is dimly aware of Saul. He's donned his green hospital scrubs. They wouldn't let him wear his Detroit Tigers baseball cap in here. He's holding her hand and his eyes are anxious with nervous energy. He thinks he's coaching her. But he keeps miscounting the breaths, and she has to correct him.

After two hours of this, she is moved into the huge circular incandescence of the delivery room. She feels as if she's about to expel her entire body outward in a floorflood. With her hair soaked with sweat and sticking to the back of her neck, she can feel the universe sputtering out for an instant into two flattened dimensions. Everything she sees is suddenly painted on a wall. She screams. Then she swears and loosens her hand from Saul's — his touch maddens her — and swears again. The pain blossoms and blossoms, a huge multicolored floral sprouting of it. When the nurses smile, the smiles — full of professionalism and complacency from the other world — make her furious. The seconds split.

"Okay, here's the head. One last push, please."

Patsy backstrokes through the pain. Then the baby girl presents herself in a mess of blood and fleshy wrappings. After the cord is cut, Patsy hears her daughter's cry and a thud to her right: Saul, on the floor, passed out, gone.

"Can someone see to the dad?" the obstetrician asks, rather calmly. "He's fainted." Then, as an afterthought, she says, "No offense, Patsy, but he looked like the fainting type."

After a moment, during which Patsy feels plumbed out and vacant, they give the baby an Apgar test. While they weigh her, a nurse squats down next to Saul and takes his pulse. "Yes, he's coming back," she says. "He'll be fine." His eyes open, and underneath the face mask he smiles sheepishly. The papery cotton over his mouth crinkles upward. It's typical of Saul, Patsy thinks, to have somebody make a fuss over him at the moment of his daughter's birth. He steals scenes.

"Is my husband okay?" she asks. She can't quite find him. Turning back to herself, she can see, blurred, in the salty recession of this birth, the paint of her toenails through her thin white cotton socks. Saul had painted those toenails when she had grown too wide to bend down and do the job herself.

"Here's the baby," the nurse says. The world has recovered itself and accordioned out into three dimensions again. The nurse's smile and her daughter's ancient sleepy expression sunspot near Patsy's heart, and the huge overhead delivery room light goes out, like a sigh.

Someone takes Patsy's hand. Who but Saul, unsteady but upright? Cold sweat drips down his forehead. He kisses Patsy through his face mask, a sterile kiss, and he informs her that they're parents now. Hi, Mom, he says. He apologizes for his cold sweat and the sudden bout of unconsciousness. Patsy raises her hand and caresses Saul's face. Oh, don't worry, the nurse says, apparently referring to Saul's fainting fit. She pats him on the back, as if he were some sort of good dog.

They name their daughter Mary Esther Carlson-Bernstein. While making dinner, one of his improvised stir-fries, Saul says that he's been having second thoughts: Mary Esther is burdened with a lot of name, a lot of Christianity and Judaism mixed in there. Possibly another name would be better. Jayne, maybe, or Liz. Direct, futuristic American monosyllables. As he theorizes and chops carrots and broccoli before dropping the bamboo shoots and water chestnuts into the pan, Patsy can see that he's so tired that he's only half-awake. His socks don't match, his jeans are beltless, and his hair has gone back to its customary anarchy.

Last night, between feedings, Saul claimed that he didn't know if he could manage it, *it* being the long haul of fatherhood. But that was just Saul-talk. Right now, Mary Esther is sleeping upstairs. Fingering the pages of her magazine, Patsy leans back in the alcove, still in her bathrobe, watching her husband cook. She wonders what she did with the breast pump and when the diaper guy is going to deliver the new batch.

Standing there, Saul sniffs, adds a spot of peanut oil, stirs again, and after a minute he ladles out dinner onto Patsy's plate. Then with that habit he has of reading her thoughts and rewording them, he turns toward her and says, "You left the breast pump upstairs." And then, "Hey, you think I'm sleepwalking. But I'm not. I'm conscious."

They live in a rented house on a dirt road outside of Five Oaks, Michigan, and for the last few months Saul has glimpsed an albino deer, always at a distance, on the fringes of their property. After work or on weekends, he walks across the unfarmed fields up to the next property line, marked by rusting fence posts, or, past the fields, into the neighboring woods of silver maple and scrub oak, hoping to get a sight of the animal. It gives him the shivers. He thinks this is the most godforsaken locale in which he's ever found himself, certainly worse than Baltimore, and that he feels right at home in it, and so does that deer. It is no easy thing to be a Jew in the Midwest, Saul thinks, where all the trees and shrubs are miserly and soul-shriveled, and where fate beats on your heart like a baseball bat, but he has mastered it. He is suited for brush and lowland undergrowth and the antipicturesque. The fungal smell of wood rot in the culverts strengthens him, he believes.

Clouds, mud, wind. Joy and despair live side by side in Saul with very few emotions in between. Even his depressions are thick with lyric intensity. In the spiritual mildew of the Midwest all winter he lives stranded in an ink drawing. He himself is the suggested figure in the lower righthand corner.

He makes his way back to the house, mud clutching fast to his boots. He has a secret he has not told Patsy, though she probably knows it: he does not have any clue to being a parent. He does not love being one, though he loves his daughter with a newfound intensity close to hysteria. To him, fatherhood is one long unrewritable bourgeois script. Love, rage, and tenderness disable him in the chairs in which he sits, miming calm, holding Mary Esther. At night, when Patsy is fast asleep, Saul kneels on the landing and beats his fists on the stairs.

On the morning when Mary Esther was celebrating her birthday — she was four weeks old — they sat at the breakfast table with the sun in a rare appearance blazing in through the east window and reflecting off the butter knife. With one hand Patsy fed herself cornflakes. With the other hand she held Mary Esther, who was nursing. Patsy was also glancing down at the morning paper on the table and was talking to Saul about his upcoming birthday, what color shirt to get him. She chewed her cornflakes thoughtfully and only reacted when Mary Esther sucked too hard. A deep brown, she says. You'd look good in that. It'd show off your eyes.

Listening, Saul watched them both, rattled by the domestic sensuality of their pairing, and his spirit shook with wild bruised jealous love. He felt pointless and redundant, an ambassador from the tiny principality of irony. His heart, that trapped bird, flapped in its cage. Behind Patsy in the kitchen the spice rack displaced its orderly contents. A delivery truck rumbled by on Whitefeather Road. He felt specifically his shallow and approximate condition. In broad daylight, night enfolded him.

He went off to work feeling superfluous and ecstatic and horny, his body glowing with its confusions.

This semester Saul has been taken off teaching American history and has been assigned remedial English for learning-disabled students in the junior high. The school claims it cannot afford a specialist in this area, and because Saul has loudly been an advocate of the rights of the learning-disabled, and because, he suspects, the principal has it in for him, he has been assigned a group of seven kids in remedial writing, and they all meet in a converted storage room at the back of the school at eight-thirty, following the second bell.

Five of them are pleasant and sweet-tempered and bewildered, but two of them hate the class and appear to hate Saul. They sit as far away from him as possible, close to the brooms, whispering to each other and smiling malevolently. Saul has tried everything with them — jokes, praise, discipline — and nothing has seemed to work.

He thinks of the two boys, Gordy Himmelman and Bob Pawlak, as the Child Cossacks. Gordy apparently has no parents. He lives with siblings and grandparents and perhaps he coalesced out of the mud of the earth. He wears tee-shirts spotted with blood and manure. His boots are scuffed from the objects he has kicked. On his face there are two rashes, one of acne, the other of blankness. His eyes, on those occasions when they meet Saul's, are cold and lunar. If you were dying on the side of the road in a rainstorm, Gordy's eyes would pass over you and continue on to the next interesting sight.

He has no sense of humor. Bob Pawlak does. He brags about killing animals, and his laughter, describing how he has killed them, rises from chuckles to a sort of rhythmic squeal. His smile is the meanest one Saul has ever seen on an ex-child. It is also visible on the face of Bob Pawlak's father. About his boy, this father has said, "Yeah, he is sure a hell-raiser." He shook his dismayed parental head, smiling meanly at Saul in the school's front office, his eyes glittering with what Saul assumed was Jew-hatred.

Saul can hardly stand to look at Gordy and Bob. There are no windows in the room where he teaches them, and no fan, and after half an hour of everyone's mingled breathing, the air in the room is foul enough to kill a canary.

Yesterday Saul gave the kids pictures clipped from magazines. They were supposed to write a one-sentence story to accompany each picture. For these ninth-graders, the task is a challenge. Now, before school starts, his mind still on Patsy and Mary Esther, Saul begins to read yesterday's sentences. Gordy and Bob have as usual not written anything: Gordy tore his picture to bits, and Bob shredded and ate his.

> It is dangerous to drive into a pool of water without the nolige of the depth because if it is salow you could hit your head that might creat unconsheness and drownding.
> Quite serprisingly the boy finds among the presents rapings which are now discarded into trash a model air plan.

Two sentences, each one requiring ten minutes' work. Saul stares at them, feeling himself stumbling in the usual cognitive limp. The sentences are like glimpses into the shattered mind of God.

> Like the hourse a cow is an animal and the human race feasts on its meat and diary which form the bulky hornd animal.
> The cold blooded crecher the bird will lay an egg and in a piriod of time a new bird will brake out of it as a storm of reproduction.

Saul looks up from his desk at the sputtering overhead lights and the grimy acoustic tile. It is in the storm of reproduction — mouths of babes, etc. — that he himself is currently being tossed.

He looks down at the floor again and spots a piece of paper with the words *your a kick* close to the wastebasket. Finally, a nice compliment. He tosses it away.

The neighbors bring food down Whitefeather Road, indented with the patterned tire-tracked mud of spring, to Saul and Patsy's house. They've read Mary Esther's birth announcement in *The Five Oaks Gazette*, but they might know anyway. Small-city snooping keeps everyone informed. With the gray March overcast behind her, Mrs. O'Neill, beaming fixedly with her brand of insane charity, offers them a plate of the cookies for which she has gained local notoriety. They look like molasses blasted in a kiln and crystallized into teeth-shattering candied rock. Anne McPhee gives Patsy a gallon of homemade potato salad preserved in pink translucent Tupperware. Laurie Welch brings molded green Jell-O. Mad Dog Bettermine hauls a case of discount no-name beer into the living room, roaring approval of the baby. In return, Saul gives Mad Dog a cigar, and together the two men retire to the back porch, lighting up and drinking, belching smoke. Back in town, Harold, Saul's barber, gives Saul a free terrible haircut. Charity is everywhere, specific and ungrudging. Saul can make no sense of it.

They all track mud into the nursery. Fond wishes are expressed. Dressed in her sleep suit, Mary Esther lies in the rickety crib that Saul himself assembled, following the confusing and contradictory instructions enclosed in the shipping box. Above the crib hangs a mobile of cardboard stars and planets. Mary Esther sleeps and cries while the mobile slowly turns in the small breezes caused by the visitors as they bend over the baby.

One night, when Mary Esther is eight weeks old and the smell of spring is pouring into the room from the purple lilacs in the driveway, Patsy awakens and finds herself alone in bed. The clock says that it's three-thirty. Saul has to be up for work in three hours. From downstairs she hears very faintly the sound of groans and music. The groans aren't Saul's. She knows his groans. These are different. She puts on her bathrobe.

In the living room, sitting in his usual overstuffed chair and wearing his blue jeans and tee-shirt, Saul is watching a porn film on the VCR. His head is propped against his arm as if he were listening attentively to a lecture. He glances up at Patsy, flashes her a guilty wave with his left hand, then returns his gaze to the movie. On the TV screen, two people, a man and a woman are having showy sex in a curiously grim manner inside a stalled freight elevator, as if they were under orders.

"What's this, Saul?"

"Film I rented."

"Where'd you get it?"

"The store."

Moans have been dubbed onto the soundtrack. The man and the woman do not look at each other. For some reason, a green ceramic poodle sits in the opposite corner of the elevator. "Not very classy, Saul," she says.

"Well," Saul says, "they're just acting." He points at the screen. "She hasn't taken her shoes off. That's pretty strange. They're having sex in the elevator and her shoes are still on. I guess the boys in the audience don't like feet."

Patsy studies the TV screen. Unexpected sadness locates her and settles in, like a headache. She rests her eyes on the Matisse poster above Saul's chair: naked people dancing in a ring. In this room the human body is excessively represented, and for a moment Patsy has the feeling that everything in life is probably too much, there is just too much to face down.

"Come upstairs, Saul."

"In a minute, after this part."

"I don't like to look at them. I don't like you looking at them."

"It's hell, isn't it?"

She touches his shoulder. "This is sort of furtive."

"That's marriage-driven rhetoric you're using there, Patsy."

"Why are you doing this, Saul?"

"Well, I wanted a real movie and I got this instead. I was in the video place and I went past the musicals into the sad private room where the Xs were. There I was, me, full of curiosity."

"About what?"

"Well, we used to have fun. We used to get hot. So this . . . anyway, it's like nostalgia, you know? Nostalgia for something. It's sort of like going into a museum where the exhibits are happy, and you watch the happiness, and it isn't yours, so you watch more of it."

"This isn't like you, Saul. Doesn't it make you feel like shit or something?"

He sits in his chair, thinking. Then he says, "Yup, it does." He clicks off the TV set, rises, and puts his arms around Patsy, and they stand quietly there for what seems to Patsy a long time. Behind Saul on the living room bookshelf are volumes of history and literature — Saul's collections of Dashiell Hammett and Samuel Eliot Morison — and the Scrabble game on the top shelf. "Don't leave me alone back here," Patsy says. "Don't leave me alone, okay?"

"I love you, Patsy," he says. "You know that. Always have."

"That's not what I'm talking about."

"I know."

"You don't get everything now," she says. "You need to diversify."

They stand for a few moments longer, swaying slightly together.

Two nights later, Saul finishes diapering Mary Esther and then walks into the upstairs hallway toward the bathroom. He brushes against Patsy, who is heading downstairs. Under the ceiling light her eyes are shadowed with fatigue. They do not speak, and for ten seconds, she is a stranger to him. He cannot remember why he married her, and he cannot remember his desire for her. He stands there, staring at the floor, angry and frightened, hoarding his injuries.

When Saul enters his classroom the next day, Gordy and Bob greet his arrival with rattled throat noises. On their foreheads they have written MAD IN THE USA, in pencil. "Mad" or "made," misspelled? Saul doesn't ask. Seated in their broken desks and only vaguely attentive, the other students fidget and smile politely, picking at their frayed clothes uniformly one or two sizes too small.

"Today," Saul says, "we're going to pretend that we're young again. We're going to think about what babies would say if they could talk."

He reaches into his jacket pocket for his seven duplicate photographs of Mary Esther, in which she leans against the back of the sofa, her stuffed gnome in her lap.

"This is my daughter," Saul says, passing the photographs out. "Mary Esther." The four girls in the classroom make peculiar cooing sounds. The boys react with nervous laughter, except for Gordy and Bob, who have suddenly turned to stone. "Babies want to say things, right? What would she say if she could talk? Write it out on a sheet of paper. Give her some words."

Saul knows he is testing the Cossacks. He is screwing up their heads with his paternal love. At the back of the room, Gordy Himmelman studies the photograph. His face expresses nothing. All his feelings are bricked up; nothing escapes from him.

His is the zombie point of view.

Nevertheless, he now bends down over his desk, pencil in hand.

At the end of the hour, Saul collects the papers, and his students shuffle out into the hallway. Saul has noticed that poor readers do not lift their feet off the floor. You can hear them coming down the hallway from the slide and scrape and squeal of their shoes.

He searches for Gordy Himmelman's paper. Here it is, mad in America, several lines of scrawled writing.

> They thro me up in to the air. Peopl come in when I screem and thro me up in to the air. They stik my face up. They never catch me.

The next lines are heavily erased.

> her   +   try it out   .   You ink

Saul holds up the paper to read the illegible words, and now he sees the word *kick* again, next to the word *lidle*.

His head randomly swimming, Saul holds the photographs of his daughter, the little kike thoughtfully misspelled by Gordy Himmelman, and brings the photos to his chest absentmindedly. From the hallway he hears the sound of lively laughter.

That night, Saul, fortified with Mad Dog's no-brand beer, reads the want ads, deeply interested. The want ads are full of trash and leavings, employment opportunities and the promise of new lives amid the advertised wreckage of the old. He reads the personals like a scholar, checking for verbal nuance. Sitting in his overstuffed chair, he scans the columns when his eye stops.

> BEEHIVES FOR SALE — Must sell. Shells, frames, extractor. Also incl. smoke and protective hat tools and face covering. Good condition. Any offer considered. Eager to deal. $$$ potential. Call after 7 P.M. 890-7236.

Saul takes Mary Esther out of her pendulum chair and holds her as he walks around the house, thick with plans and vision. In the vision, he stands proudly — regally! — in front of Patsy, holding a jar of honey. Sunlight slithers through its glass and transforms the room itself into pure gold. Sweetness is everywhere. Honey will make all the desires right again between them. Gordy Himmelman, meanwhile, will have erased himself from the planet. He will have caused himself to disappear. Patsy accepts Saul's gift. She can't stop smiling at him. She tears off their clothes. She pours the honey over Saul.

Gazing at the newspapers and magazines piling up next to the TV set as he holds Mary Esther, Saul finds himself shaking with a kind of excitement. Irony, his constant companion, is asleep, or on vacation, and in the heady absence of irony Saul begins to imagine himself as a beekeeper.

He does not accuse Gordy of anti-Semitism, or of anything else. He ignores him, as he ignores Bob Pawlak. At the end of the school year they will go away and fall down into the earth and the dirt they came from and become one with the stones and the inanimate all-embracing horizon.

On a fine warm day in April, Saul drives out to the north side of town, where he buys the wooden frames and the other equipment from a laconic man named Gunderson. Gunderson wears overalls and boots. Using the flat of his hand, he rubs the top of his bald head with a farmer's gesture of suspicion as he examines Saul's white shirt, pressed pants, ten-day growth of beard, and brown leather shoes. "Don't wear black clothes around these fellas," Gunderson advises. "They hate black." Saul pays him in cash, and Gunderson counts the money after Saul has handed it over, wetting his thumb to turn the bills.

With Mad Dog's pickup, Saul brings it all back to Whitefeather Road. He stores his purchases behind the garage. He takes out books on beekeeping from the public library and studies their instructions with care. He takes notes in a yellow notebook and makes calculations about placement. The bees need direct sunlight, and water nearby. By long-distance telephone he buys a hive of bees, complete with a queen, from an apiary in South Carolina, using his credit card number. When the bee box arrives in the main post office, he receives an angry call from the assistant postal manager telling him to come down and pick up this damn humming thing.

As it turns out, the bees like Saul. He is calm and slow around them and talks to them when he removes them from the shipping box and introduces them into the shells and frames, following the instructions that he has learned by heart. The hives and frames sit unsteadily on the platform Saul has laid down on bricks near two fence posts on the edge of the property. But the structure is, he thinks, steady enough for bees. He gorges them with sugar syrup, sprinkling it over them, before letting them free, shaking them into the frames. Some of them settle on his gloved hand and are so drowsy that, when he pushes them off, they waterfall into the hive. When the queen and the other bees are enclosed, he replaces the frames inside the shell, being careful to put a feeder with sugar water nearby.

The books have warned him about the loud buzzing sound of angry bees, but for the first few days Saul never hears it. Something about Saul seems to keep the bees occupied and unirritated. He is stung twice, once on the wrist and once on the back of the neck, but the pain is pointed and directed and so focused that he can manage it. It's unfocused pain that he can't stand.

Out at the back of Saul's property, a quarter mile away from the house, the hives and the bees won't bother anyone, Saul thinks. "Just don't bring them in here," Patsy tells him, glancing through one of his apiary books. "Not that they'd come. I just want them and me to have a little distance between us, is all." She smiles. "Bees, Saul? Honey? You're such a literalist."

And then one night, balancing his checkbook at his desk, with Mary Esther half asleep in the crook of his left arm, Saul feels a moment of calm peacefulness, the rarest of his emotions. Under his desk lamp, with his daughter burping up on his Johns Hopkins sweatshirt, he sits forward, waiting. He turns around and sees Patsy, in worn jeans and a tee-shirt, watching him from the doorway. Her arms are folded, and her breasts are outlined perfectly beneath the cloth. She is holding on her face an expression of sly playfulness. He thinks she looks beautiful and tells her so.

She comes into the room, her bare feet whisking against the wood floor, and she puts her arms around him, pressing herself against him.

"Put Mary Esther into her crib," she whispers. She clicks off the desk lamp.

As they make love, Saul thinks of his bees. Those insects, he thinks, are a kind of solution.

Spring moves into summer, and the mud on Whitefeather Road dries into sculpted gravel. Just before school ends, Saul tells his students about the bees and the hives. Pride escapes from his face, radiating it. When he explains how honey is extracted from the frames, he glances at Gordy Himmelman and sees a look of dumb animal rage directed back at him. The boy looks as if he's taking a bath in lye. What's the big deal? Saul wonders before he turns away.

One night in early June, Patsy is headed upstairs, looking for the Snugli, which she thinks she forgot in Mary Esther's room, when she hears Saul's voice coming from behind the door. She stops on the landing, her hand on the banister. At first she thinks he might be singing to Mary Esther, but, no, Saul is not singing. He's sitting in there — well, he's probably sitting, Saul doesn't like to stand when he speaks — talking to his daughter, and Patsy hears him finishing a sentence: ". . . was never very happy."

Patsy moves closer to the door.

"Who explains?" Saul is saying, apparently to his daughter. "No one."

Saul goes on talking to Mary Esther, filling her in on his mother and several other mysterious phenomena. What does he think he's doing, discussing this stuff with an infant? "I should sing you a song," he announces, interrupting himself. "That's what parents do."

To get away from Saul's song, Patsy retreats to the window for a breath of air. Looking out, she sees someone standing on the front lawn, bathed in moonlight, staring in the direction of the house. He's thin and ugly and scruffy, and he looks a bit like a clod, but a dangerous clod.

"Saul," she says. Then, more loudly, "Saul, there's someone out on the lawn."

He joins her at the window. "I can't see him," Saul says. "Oh, yeah, there." He shouts, "Hello? Can I help you?"

The boy turns around. "Sure, fuckwad. Yeah, you bet, shitbird." He gets on a bike and races away down the driveway and onto Whitefeather Road.

Saul does not move. His hands are planted on the windowsill. "It's Gordy Himmelman," he groans. "That little bastard has come on our property. I'm getting on the phone."

"Saul, why'd he come here? What did you do to him?" She holds her arms against her chest. "What does he have against us?"

"I was his teacher. And we're Jewish," Saul says. "And, uh, we're parents. He never had any. I showed those kids the baby pictures. Big mistake. Somebody must've found Gordy somewhere in a barrel of brine. He was not of woman born." He tries to smile. "I'm kidding, sort of."

"Do you think he'll be back?" she asks.

"Oh yes." Saul wipes his forehead. "They always come back, those kind. And I'll be ready."

It has been a spring and summer of violent weather, and Saul has been reading the Old Testament again, looking for clues. On Thursday, at four in the afternoon, Saul has finished mowing the front lawn and is sitting on the porch drinking the last bottle of Mad Dog's beer when he looks to the west and feels a sudden cooling of the air, a shunting of atmospheres. Just above the horizon a mass of clouds begins boiling. Clouds that look like breasts and handtools — he can't help thinking the way he thinks — advance over him. The wind picks up.

"Patsy," he calls. "Hey Patsy."

Something calamitous is happening in the atmosphere. The pressure is dropping so fast that Saul can feel it in his elbows and knees.

"Patsy!" he shouts.

From upstairs he hears her calling back, "What, Saul?"

"Go to the basement," he says. "Close the upstairs window and take Mary Esther down there. Take a flashlight. We're going to get a huge storm."

Through the house Saul rushes, closing windows and switching off lights, and when he returns to the front door to close it, he sees in the front yard the tall and emaciated apparition of Gordy Himmelman, standing fixedly like an emanation from the dirt and stone of the fields. He has returned. Toward Saul he aims his vacant stare. Saul, who cannot stop thinking even in moments of critical emergency, is struck into stillness by Gordy's presence, his authoritative malevolence standing there in the just mown grass. The volatile ambitious sky and the forlorn backwardness of the fields have together given rise to this human disaster, who, even as Saul watches, yells toward the house, "Hey, Mr. Bernstein. Guess what. Just guess what. Go take a look at your bees."

Feeling like a commando, Saul, who is fast when he has to be, catches up to Gordy who is pumping away on his broken and rusted bicycle. Saul tears

Gordy off. He throws and kicks the junk Schwinn into the ditch. In the rain that has just started, Saul grabs Gordy by the shoulders and shakes him back and forth. He presses his thumbs hard enough to bruise. Gordy, violently stinking, smells of neglect and seepage, and Saul nearly gags. Saul cannot stop shaking him. He cannot stop shaking himself. With violent rapid horizontal jerking motions the boy's head is whipped.

Saul wants to see his eyes. But the eyes are as empty as mirrors.

"Hey, stop it," Gordy says. "It hurts. You're hurting. You're hurting him."

"Hurt who?" Saul asks. Thunder rolls toward him. He sees himself reflected in Gordy Himmelman's eyes, a tiny figure backed by lightning. *Who, me?*

"Stop it, don't hurt him." Patsy's voice, repeating Gordy's words, snakes into his ear, and he feels her hand on his arm, restraining him. She's here, out in this rain, less frightened of the rain than she is of Saul. The boy has started to sag, seeing the two of them there, his scarecrow arms raised to protect himself, assuming, probably, that he's about to be killed. There he squats, the child of attention deficit, at Saul's feet.

"Stay there," Saul mumbles. "Stay right there." Through the rain he begins walking, then running, toward his bees.

The storm, empty of content, tucks itself toward the east and is being replaced even now by one of those insincere Midwestern blue skies.

Mary Esther begins to cry and wail as Patsy jogs toward Saul. Gordy Himmelman follows along behind her.

When she is within a hundred feet of Saul's beehives, she sees that the frames have been knocked over, scattered, and kicked. Saul lies, face down, where they once stood. He is touching his tongue to the earth momentarily, where the honey is, for a brief taste. When he rises, he sees Patsy. "All the bees swarmed," he says. "They've left. They're gone."

She holds Mary Esther tightly and examines Saul's face. "How come they didn't attack him? Didn't they sting him?"

"Who knows?" Saul spreads his arms. "They just didn't."

Gordy Himmelman watches them from a hundred yards away, and with his empty gaze he makes Patsy think of the albino deer Saul has insisted he has seen: half blind, wandering these fields day after day without direction.

"Look," Saul says, pointing at Mary Esther, who stopped crying when she saw her father. "Her shoe is untied." He wipes his face with his sleeve and shakes off the dirt from his jeans. Approaching Patsy, he gives off a smell of dirt and honey and sweat. In the midst of his distractedness, he ties Mary Esther's shoe.

His hair is soaked with rain. He glances at Patsy, who, with some difficulty, is keeping her mouth shut. She not only loves Saul but at this moment is in love with him, and she has to be careful not to say so just now. It's strange, she thinks, that she loves him, an odd trick of fate: He is fitful and emotional, a man whose sense of theater begins completely with himself. What she loves is the extravagance of feeling that focuses itself into the tiniest actions of human attention, like the tying of this pink shoe. It's better to keep love a secret for a while than to talk about it all the time. It generates more energy that way. He finishes the knot. He kisses them both. Dirt is attached to his lips.

At a distance of a hundred yards, the boy, Gordy, watches all this, and from her vantage point Patsy cannot guess what that expression on his face may mean, those mortuary eyes. Face it: He's a loss. Whatever they have to give away, they can only give him a tiny portion, and it won't be enough, whatever it is. All the same, he will stick around, she's pretty sure of that. They will have to give him something, because now, like it or not, he's following them back, their faithful zombie, made, or mad, in America, and now he's theirs.

Well, maybe we're missionaries, Patsy thinks, as she stumbles and Saul holds her up. We're the missionaries they left behind when they took all the religion away. On the front porch of the house she can see the empty bottle of Saul's no-brand beer still standing on the lip of the ledge, and she can see the porch swing slowly rock back and forth, as if someone were sitting there, waiting for them.

Gravity

KIM ADDONIZIO

Carrying my daughter to bed
I remember how light she once was,
no more than a husk in my arms.
There was a time I could not put her down,
so frantic was her crying if I tried
to pry her from me, so I held her
for hours at night, walking up and down the hall,
willing her to fall asleep. She'd grow quiet,
pressed against me, her small being alert
to each sound, the tension in my arms, she'd take
my nipple and gaze up at me,
blinking back fatigue she'd fight whatever terror
waited beyond my body in her dark crib. Now
that she's so heavy I stagger beneath her,
she slips easily from me, down
into her own dreaming. I stand over her bed,
fixed there like a second, dimmer star,
though the stars are not fixed: someone
once carried the weight of my life.

Orangutan Means Orange Man

DEBORAH DIGGES

The oldest faces us, sidesteps his way
along the inner cage edge, his beautiful long
arms extended, his big hands open.
He's begging, says a visitor,
though he doesn't stop to pick up what he
cannot catch, and what he can he tosses back to us.
He's showing off, says a visitor, and turns
in sudden bored contempt
not to be compared with the orangutan's.
I remember the dead assenting eyes of old men
in depots who play for hand-outs harmonicas
and combs — how once when I tossed a quarter
onto their filthy army blanket, one of them lifted
his long coat to show me, angry, one leg
bound from his knee against his thigh.
I've thought since then that late at night,
both his good legs stretched out on a bare mattress,
the ache must gratify the crime.
I must have turned, wearing the slouched,
submissive grin of the human animal,
the one I've learned to use on buses, in subways,
where I've heard the European tunnels echo
with street musicians playing Schumann, Mozart.
As I make my way through those corridors
once used as air raid shelters
toward the right train home, glad to be
going and at the same time trapped in the beauty
of that flute or violin, I can't help thinking

how, to stay alive in Belsen,
the best musicians had to play on night and day,
even as their families were herded past them.
The train door closes and I avoid my reflection,
avoid that terrible empathy
that turns one suddenly into everyone's guardian.
—I've sat whole days with my babies,
examining as does the female here,
their little bodies, picking off the dusty slough,
like sunburned skin, left over from the womb,
smoothing their hair, sleeping when they sleep,
inhaling easily their strong, milky expulsions.
It was that trance I moved from finally,
as from a closed room into sunlight,
but I was changed, changed. Changed irrevocably.

Prayer for My Children

KATE DANIELS

I regret nothing.
My cruelties, my betrayals
of others I once thought
I loved. All the unlived
years, the unwritten
poems, the wasted nights
spent weeping and drinking.

No, I regret nothing
because what I've lived
has led me here, to this room
with its marvelous riches,
its simple wealth —
these three heads shining
beneath the Japanese lamp, laboring
over crayons and paper.
These three who love me
exactly as I am, precisely
at the center of my ill-built being.
Who rear up eagerly when I enter,
and fall down weeping when I leave.
Whose eyes are my eyes.
Hair, my hair.
Whose bodies I cover
with kisses and blankets.
Whose first meal was my own body.
Whose last, please God, I will not live
to serve, or share.

Now That I Am Forever with Child

AUDRE LORDE

How the days went
while you were blooming within me
I remember   each upon each
the swelling changed planes of my body

how you first fluttered   then jumped
and I thought it was my heart.

How the days wound down
and the turning of winter
I recall   you
growing heavy against the wind.
I thought   now her hands
are formed   her hair
has started to curl
now her teeth are done
now she sneezes.

Then the seed opened.
I bore you one morning
just before spring
my head rang like a fiery piston
my legs were towers between which
a new world was passing.

Since then
I can only distinguish
one thread within running hours
you   flowing through selves
toward You.

Contributors

Kim Addonizio's three collections of poetry include *Tell Me*, which was a 2000 National Book Award finalist. With Dorianne Laux she coauthored *The Poet's Companion: A Guide to the Pleasures of Writing Poetry*.

Margaret Atwood is the author of more than twenty-five books, including fiction, poetry, and essays. Her most recent works include the bestselling novels *The Blind Assassin*, *Alias Grace*, and *The Robber Bride*, and the collections *Wilderness Tips* and *Good Bones* and *Simple Murders*. She lives in Toronto.

Jimmy Santiago Baca entered, illiterate, a maximum-security prison at the age of twenty-one; he emerged five years later with a passion for poetry. His many collections include *Healing Earthquakes*, *Black Mesa Poems*, and *Immigrants in Our Own Land*. He has recently published his memoir, *A Place to Stand*.

Julianna Baggott has written three novels, *Girl Talk*, *The Miss America Family*, and *The Madam*, as well as a book of poems, *This Country of Mothers*. Her poems and stories have appeared in *Poetry*, *Ms.*, the *Southern Review*, and *Best American Poetry 2000*.

Charles Baxter's most recent novel, *The Feast of Love*, was a finalist for the National Book Award. He has published two other novels, *First Light* and *Shadow Play*, and four books of stories, most recently *Believers*. He teaches at the University of Michigan, Ann Arbor.

Eavan Boland was born in Ireland and has published eight volumes of poetry, including *Outside History* and *The Lost Land*. Her memoir, *Object Lessons: The Life of a Woman Poet in Our Time*, received the Lannan Foundation Award. She directs the creative writing program at Stanford University.

Rosemary Bray has been a writer and editor for *Ms.*, *Essence*, and the *New York Times Sunday Book Review*. She is the author of two books: *Martin Luther King*, a children's biography, and the critically acclaimed memoir *Unafraid of the Dark*. She is an ordained Unitarian Universalist minister in New York City.

A. S. Byatt's works of fiction include *Possession*, winner of the Booker Prize in 1990, the sequence *The Virgin in the Garden*, *Still Life* (excerpted in this book), *Babel Tower*, and, most recently, *The Biographer's Tale*. She is also the author of several important critical works and a collection of essays, *Passions of the Mind*.

Jim Daniels's books include *Night with Drive-By Shooting Stars*, *Blessing the House*, *M-80*, and *No Pets*, a collection of stories. He also edited *Letters to America: Contemporary American Poetry about Race*, and he coedited *American Poetry: The Next Generation*.

Kate Daniels is the author of *The White Wave*, winner of the Agnes Lynch Starrett Poetry Prize; *The Niobe Poems*; and *Four Testimonies*. She is the coeditor of a volume of critical essays on Robert Bly, *Of Solitude and Silence*, and the editor of Muriel Rukeyser's selected poems, *Out of Silence*.

Corinne Demas (aka Corinne Demas Bliss) teaches at Mt. Holyoke College and is a fiction editor of the *Massachusetts Review*. She is the author of two story collections, two novels, the memoir *Eleven Stories High: Growing Up in Stuyvesant Town, 1948–68*, and numerous children's books.

Toi Derricotte has published four collections of poetry—*Natural Birth*, *The Empress of the Death House*, *Captivity*, and *Tender*—and one work of nonfiction, *The Black Notebooks*. With Cornelius Eady, she founded Cave Canem, the first workshop retreat for African American poets.

Deborah Digges's most recent book is *The Stardust Lounge: Stories from a Boy's Adolescence*, and she is the author of the poetry collections *Rough Music* and *Vesper Sparrows*, and the memoir, *Fugitive Spring*. She teaches at Tufts University.

Stephen Dobyns has published ten books of poems, twenty novels, a book of essays on poetry, *Best Words, Best Order*, and a book of short stories, *Eating Naked*. His most recent book of poems is *Pallbearers Envying the One Who Rides*. He lives with his family near Boston.

Rita Dove served as Poet Laureate of the United States and Consultant to the Library of Congress from 1993 to 1995. She received the 1987 Pulitzer Prize in Poetry for *Thomas and Beulah*. Other books include *Grace Notes*, *Selected Poems*, and *Mother Love*. She lives in Charlottesville, Virginia, with her husband and daughter.

Stephen Dunn is the author of eleven collections of poetry, including *Different Hours*, winner of the 2001 Pulitzer Prize.

Elyse Gasco lives in Montreal and has degrees in creative writing from Concordia University and New York University. She received the Journey Prize, Canada's most prestigious award for short fiction, for *Can You Wave Bye Bye, Baby?*

Louise Glück's *The Wild Iris* received the 1992 Pulitzer Prize for poetry. Other collections include *Seven Ages, Vita Nova, Meadowlands, Ararat,* and *The Triumph of Achilles,* which received the National Book Critics Circle Award. She teaches at Williams College and lives in Cambridge, Massachusetts.

Jesse Green is an award-winning journalist and a regular contributor to the *New York Times Magazine.* He is the author of the novel *O Beautiful* and the memoir *The Velveteen Father: An Unexpected Journey to Parenthood.*

Mary Grimm teaches writing at Case Western Reserve University. Her short fiction, collected in *Stealing Time,* has appeared in *Redbook, Story,* and *The New Yorker,* and has been selected for a National Magazine Award and *Best American Short Stories.* Grimm is also the author of a novel, *Left to Themselves.*

Hunt Hawkins chairs the English department at Florida State University. His book of poems, *The Domestic Life,* won the 1992 Agnes Lynch Starrett Poetry Prize. His poems have appeared in *Poetry,* the *Georgia Review,* the *Southern Review, TriQuarterly,* the *Minnesota Review,* and many other journals.

Edward Hirsch, a 1998 MacArthur Fellow, has published five books of poems, including *Earthly Measures* and *On Love.* He has also published two prose books, *Responsive Reading* and *How to Read a Poem and Fall in Love with Poetry,* a national bestseller. He teaches at the University of Houston.

Harry Humes's most recent poetry collections are *The Bottomland* and *Butterfly Effect,* selected by Pattiann Rogers for the 1998 National Poetry Series. He has been a recipient of several Pennsylvania Council on the Arts grants and a National Endowment for the Arts fellowship in poetry.

Galway Kinnell is a former MacArthur Fellow and state poet of Vermont. In 1982 his *Selected Poems* won the Pulitzer Prize and the National Book Award. He has translated the works of Bonnefoy, Lorca, Rilke, and Villon. He lives in New York City and Vermont.

Gary Krist has published two novels—*Chaos Theory* and *Bad Chemistry*—and two short-story collections—*The Garden State* and *Bone by Bone.* A regular book reviewer, travel writer, and op-ed page satirist, he lives in Bethesda, Maryland, with his wife and daughter.

Laurie Kutchins wrote *The Night Path* and *Between Towns*. She is working on a third book of poems and a multigenre book on weather and narrative, raising two children, teaching poetry at James Madison University, and yes, her house is not immaculate.

Li-Young Lee was born in Jakarta, Indonesia, and now lives in Chicago with his wife and two sons. He is the author of three books of poems, *Rose*, *The City in Which I Love You*, and *Book of My Nights*, and a book-length autobiographical prose poem, *The Winged Seed*.

Lisa Lenzo's story collection, *Within the Lighted City*, was chosen by Ann Beattie for the 1997 John Simmons Short Fiction Award. Her stories have been anthologized in *The Iowa Award: The Best Stories, 1991–2000*; *Sacred Ground: Stories about Home*; and *The Portable Italian-American*.

Phillip Lopate has collected his essays in eight books, including *Bachelorhood, Against Joie de Vivre*, and *Portrait of My Body*. He is the editor of *The Art of the Personal Essay*, *The Anchor Essay Annual*, and *Writing New York: A Literary Anthology*. He lives in Brooklyn, New York, with his wife and daughter.

Audre Lorde (1934–1992) established herself, over a prolific career, as a poet and activist in the causes of black American culture, gay rights, and feminism. Her poems are collected in *Undersong*. She chronicled her battle against breast cancer in *The Cancer Journals*.

Thomas Lux directs the MFA program in poetry at Sarah Lawrence College. A former Guggenheim fellow, he received the Kingsly Tufts Award for *Split Horizon*, and his *New and Selected Poems: 1975–1995* was shortlisted for both the Poet's Prize and the Lenore Marshall / The Nation Award. His latest book is *The Street of Clocks*.

Jane McCafferty teaches fiction and nonfiction at Carnegie Mellon University in Pittsburgh. Her book of stories, *Director of the World*, won the Drue Heinz Literature Prize, and her novel, *One Heart*, was a Book Sense Bestseller.

Campbell McGrath, author of five books of poetry, including *Florida Poems* and *Spring Comes to Chicago*, has received fellowships from the Guggenheim and MacArthur Foundations. He lives with his family in Miami Beach.

Gary Metras's poems, essays, and reviews appear in *The American Voice, Boston Review of Books, Connecticut Poetry Review, Poetry, Poetry East,* and *Yankee.* He is the father of two who are about to leave the nest.

David Mura has published two books of poetry, *The Colors of Desire* and *After We Lost Our Way,* and two memoirs, *Where the Body Meets Memory* and *Turning Japanese. Notes for a New Century,* a book of poetry criticism, is forthcoming.

Sharon Olds's books are *Satan Says, The Dead and the Living, The Gold Cell, The Father, The Wellspring,* and *Blood, Tin, Straw.* She teaches in the graduate program in creative writing at New York University and helps run the NYU writing workshop at a state hospital for the severely physically challenged.

Alicia Ostriker has published nine volumes of poetry, including *The Imaginary Lover,* which won the 1986 William Carlos Williams Award, and *The Crack in Everything,* a National Book Award finalist. Her latest volume is *The Volcano Sequence.*

Linda Pastan's *Carnival Evening: New and Selected Poems, 1968–1998* was a finalist for the National Book Award. *The Last Uncle,* her eleventh book of poems, appeared in 2002.

Sylvia Plath (1932–1963) published one book of poems, *The Colossus,* prior to her suicide at age thirty. *Ariel, Crossing the Water,* and *Winter Trees* were published posthumously, and her *Collected Poems* received the Pulitzer Prize in 1982.

Eileen Pollack is the author of a collection of short fiction, *The Rabbi in the Attic and Other Stories;* a novel, *Paradise, New York;* and a book-length work of creative nonfiction, *Woman Walking Ahead: In Search of Catherine Weldon and Sitting Bull.* She teaches at the University of Michigan.

Lia Purpura's first collection of essays, *Increase,* won the Associated Writing Programs Award in Creative Nonfiction. Her collection of poems, *Stone Sky Lifting,* won the OSU Press / *The Journal* Award. She teaches at Loyola College in Baltimore, where she lives with her husband and son.

Herbert Scott is the founder and editor of New Issues Poetry and Prose books, and he teaches at Western Michigan University. His published work includes the books *Disguises, Groceries, Durations,* and *In the Palm of Space.*

Gary Snyder is a poet, essayist, mountaineer, and Buddhist ecologist. He lives in the California Sierra, just north of the South Yuba River. His most recent book is *The Gary Snyder Reader*.

Cathy Song lives in Honolulu. She is the author of *Picture Bride, Frameless Windows, Squares of Light, School Figures*, and her most recent collection of poems, *The Land of Bliss*.

Elizabeth Spires is the author of five books of poems: *Globe, Swan's Island, Annonciade, Worldling*, and *Now the Green Blade Rises*. She has also written five books for children, including *The Mouse of Amherst, I Am Arachne*, and *Riddle Road*. She lives in Baltimore and teaches at Goucher College.

Ann Townsend's first collection of poetry, *Dime Store Erotics*, won the Gerald Cable Prize. Her poems, stories, and essays have appeared in such magazines as *Poetry*, the *Nation*, the *Paris Review*, and the *Southern Review*. She lives in Denison, Ohio, with her husband and daughter, and she teaches at Denison University.

Quincy Troupe has written thirteen books, the latest of which are *Avalanche* and *Choruses*. He is the coauthor (with Miles Davis) of *Miles: The Autobiography*, and the author of *Miles and Me*. *Trancircularities: New and Selected Poems* appeared in 2002. He teaches at the University of California, San Diego.

Lee Upton's four books of poetry include *Approximate Darling, No Mercy*, and *Civilian Histories*. She is also the author of three books of literary criticism, including, most recently, *The Muse of Abandonment*.

Jeanne Murray Walker's books include *Nailing Up the Home Sweet Home, Coming into History*, and *Gaining*. She has received fellowships from the National Endowment for the Arts and the Pew Charitable Trust. She lives in Philadelphia and teaches at the University of Delaware.

Belle Waring's first collection, *Refuge*, won the 1989 Associated Writing Programs Award and was cited by *Publishers Weekly* as one of the best books of 1990. Her second book of poems, *Dark Blonde*, was awarded the 1998 Larry Levis Prize. She is a commentator for National Public Radio.

Permissions

We are grateful to the authors who have given us permission to include previously unpublished work in this anthology. We also thank the authors, editors, and publishers who have given us permission to reprint their selections.

Kim Addonizio: "Gravity," from *The Philosopher's Club*, BOA Editions, Ltd. Copyright © 1994 by Kim Addonizio. Reprinted by permission of the author and BOA Editions, Ltd.

Margaret Atwood: "Giving Birth," from *Dancing Girls*, Simon and Schuster, Inc. Copyright © 1977, 1982 by O. W. Toad Ltd. Reprinted by permission of the author.

Jimmy Santiago Baca: "Child of the Sun — Gabriel's Birth (Sun Prayer)," from *Black Mesa Poems*, New Directions Publishing Corp. Copyright © 1989 by Jimmy Santiago Baca. Reprinted by permission of New Directions Publishing Corp.

Julianna Baggott: "My Mother Gives Birth" and "After Giving Birth, I Recall the Madonna and Child," from *This Country of Mothers*, Southern Illinois University Press. Copyright © 2001 by Julianna Baggott. Reprinted by permission of the author and Southern Illinois University Press.

Charles Baxter: "Saul and Patsy Are in Labor," from *Believers: A Novella and Stories*, Pantheon Books. Copyright © 1997 by Charles Baxter. Reprinted by permission of the author and Pantheon Books, a division of Random House, Inc.

Eavan Boland: "Night Feed," an excerpt from "Domestic Interior," from *An Origin Like Water: Collected Poems 1967–1987*, W. W. Norton and Company. Copyright © 1996 by Eavan Boland. Reprinted by permission of the author and W. W. Norton and Company.

Rosemary Bray: "First Stirrings," from *Minding the Body: Women Writers on Body and Soul*, ed. Patricia Foster, Anchor Books. Copyright © 1994 by Rosemary Bray. Reprinted by permission of the author.

Index

Addonizio, Kim, 239
After Giving Birth, I Recall the Madonna and Child, 84
Ancestral Lights, 113–114
Apnea, 163
Atwood, Margaret, 70–83

Babylove, 151–154
Babyshit Serenade, 166
Baca, Jimmy Santiago, 101–103
Baggott, Julianna, 55, 84
Baxter, Charles, 223–238
Before, 17–27
Birth Report, 104–105
Boland, Eavan, 179–180
Bray, Rosemary, 10–13
Breastfeeding in Indiana, 189–198
Brown Circle, 213–214
Byatt, A. S., 61–66

Changing Diapers, 165
Child of the Sun — Gabriel's Birth (Sun Prayer), 101–103
Cleaning the Pheasant in the Fifth Month of My Wife's Pregnancy, 14
Coming Home from the Hospital after My Son's Birth, 143

Daniels, Jim, 143, 199–200
Daniels, Kate, 3–4, 188, 242
Delivering Lily, 85–100

Delphos, Ohio, 28–30
Demas, Corinne, 151–154
Derricotte, Toi, 56–60
Digges, Deborah, 113–114, 240–241
Dobyns, Stephen, 104–105
Domestic Interior, from, 179–180
Dove, Rita, 216
Dunn, Stephen, 138–139

Eighteenth-Century Medical Illustration: The Infant in Its Little Room, 31–32

First Day, The, 115–116
First Pregnancy, 5
First Stirrings, 10–13
First Summer, 201–203
For Fathers of Girls, 138–139

Gas, 164
Gasco, Elyse, 38–51
Genesis 1:28, 3–4
Giving Birth, 70–83
Glück, Louise, 213–214
Gravity, 239
Green, Jesse, 156–162
Grimm, Mary, 17–27

Hawkins, Hunt, 118–119, 163
Heartbeat, 8
Her First Week, 150

Hirsch, Edward, 144–147
Holding Bernadette, 118–119
How It Begins, 117
Humes, Harry, 14

Kinnell, Galway, 207–212
Krist, Gary, 167–178
Kutchins, Laurie, 8, 201–203

Lee, Li-Young, 184–187
Lenzo, Lisa, 106–112
Letter in July, 6–7
Listening, 33–34
Little Sleep's-Head Sprouting Hair in
     the Moonlight, 207–212
Lopate, Phillip, 85–100
Lorde, Audre, 243
Lux, Thomas, 9

Man Who Would Be a Mother, The,
     155
March, 199–200
McCafferty, Jane, 189–198
McGrath, Campbell, 28–30
Ménage à trois, 188
Metras, Gary, 5
Milk, 120–137
Morning Song, 181
Motherhood, 216
Mura, David, 33–34, 117
My Mother Gives Birth, 55

New Mother, 183
Notes from the Delivery Room, 69
Now That I Am Forever with Child,
     243

Olds, Sharon, 150, 183
Orangutan Means Orange Man, 240–
     241
Ostriker, Alicia, 166, 217–222

Pastan, Linda, 69
Plath, Sylvia, 15, 181
Pollack, Eileen, 120–137
Prayer for My Children, 242
Propaganda Poem: Maybe for Some
     Young Mamas, 217–222
Purpura, Lia, 36–37

Reading the New York Times, 16
Requiem, 36–37

Saul and Patsy Are in Labor, 223–238
Scott, Herbert, 155
Shrinking the Uterus, 148–149
Simple Joys, 215
Sleep, 167–178
Snyder, Gary, 165
Song, Cathy, 35, 148–149
Sorrow, 182
Spires, Elizabeth, 6–7, 115–116
Still Life, from, 61–66

This Night, 35
Townsend, Ann, 31–32, 182
Transition, 56–60
Troupe, Quincy, 215

Upon Seeing an Ultrasound Photo of
     an Unborn Child, 9
Upton, Lee, 67–68

Velveteen Father, The, from, 156–162

Waiting, 106–112
Waiting, The, 184–187
Walker, Jeanne Murray, 16

Waring, Belle, 164
Welcoming, The, 144–147
Women's Labors, 67

You Have the Body, 38–51
You're, 15